CW00670073

SACRED SPACES

*Communion with the horse
through science and spirit*

SUSAN D. FAY, PhD

SP Selenite Press, Ltd.
Elbert, Colorado

Copyright © 2019 by Susan D. Fay, PhD

All rights reserved. No part of this publication may be reproduced, distributed or transmitted in any form or by any means, including photocopying, recording, or other electronic or mechanical methods, without the prior written permission of the publisher, except in the case of brief quotations embodied in critical reviews and certain other noncommercial uses permitted by copyright law.

The author of this book does not dispense any medical advice, diagnose any medical issue, or prescribe any therapeutic technique as a form of treatment for any physical, emotional, or medical symptom in equines or humans. A physician, mental health practitioner, veterinarian, or appropriate medical professional should be consulted for advice on treatment for any physical, mental, behavioral, or emotional condition. The intent of the author is to provide general information to assist you in your search for emotional and spiritual well-being. In the event that you use any of the information contained in this book for your personal use or instruction of others, the author assumes no responsibility for your actions or the consequences of your actions on humans or equines.

Front and Rear Cover Photos by Karen L. Duplantis, Fiore Photography
Book Cover Design by Ellen Storeim, Ellen Kendrick Creative, Inc.
Book Layout ©2017 BookDesignTemplates.com

Sacred Spaces/Susan D. Fay, PhD—1st ed.

ISBN-13: 978-0-578-44729-2

(SP   Published by Selenite Press, Ltd.
       10344 Little Moon Trail
       Elbert, Colorado 80106

Dedicated to my horses—alive and deceased—who gave me the gift of sight and guided me to the sacred space.

Communion: *the sharing or exchanging of intimate thoughts and feelings, especially when the exchange is on a mental or spiritual level.*

—Oxford Dictionaries

Contents

Acknowledgments

To my sister Nancy and her husband Ron, I am grateful for your encouragement and support. You are more than family, you are my friends. Thank you to my brother Charles for your guidance on writing a book. And to my Dad, thanks for your advice and support as I pursued my dream.

A very special thanks to my friend Rebecca Corona for giving me the strength to believe in myself. You are my sister forever.

To Sherry Celsy and Michael Finkbeiner, thank you for your friendship and for the work you do to make horses' lives better.

My utmost appreciation to Don Martinez, a cow(man), horseman, and friend without equal. You provided me with the encouragement that I needed to finish my PhD and find my way to a new life.

I extend my sincere thanks to Karen Duplantis for the beautiful photos that grace the cover of this book, and Ellen Storeim for the elegant cover design.

A big thank you to Tabitha Carver-Roberts for your book-writing and editing suggestions.

Thank you, Inez Throm, for giving me an opportunity to do one of my first *Sacred Spaces* clinics at your beautiful and tranquil ranch in Parachute, Colorado. You are an unbelievably talented horsewoman.

To my special friends and all those who have been a big part of making my journey possible: Leslie Campbell, Art and Kay Cook, Deb Donley, Medora Fralick, Susan Girten, Dr. Regan Golob, Kristen Schaugaard-Green, Dr. Karen Hanks, Carla Shelton-Knight, Lou Lueders, Jennifer Murray, Gary and Jackie Murray, Dr. Mary O'Brien, Dr. Sandra Rasmussen, Dee Stiers, Jon Tandler, Esq., Debbie Tenney, Dr. Sandra Thebaud, George and Dr. Jacklyn Wenschhof, and Gail Wild.

Preface

Frustrated, I tossed and turned in bed desperately trying to quiet the nagging voice in my head. It kept asking me over and over again, "What do you want to be when you grow up?" The answer to this question had eluded me for more than 50 years, so it seemed unlikely that I would have a revelation on this particular evening—or would I?

Lying in bed staring at the ceiling, the voice became silent for a moment as my mind began projecting sweet images of foals frolicking in the lush green grass of the White River valley.

Above the gurgle of the river, I could hear the faint sound of mama cows calling their calves. For a brief but beautiful moment, I was back at my old ranch, doing what I loved. But reality returned with a vengeance, reminding me that there was no chance anyone would consider hiring a woman of my age as a ranch hand, even though I still felt strong enough to do that kind of strenuous work.

As the images of the ranch faded, they were quickly replaced by the memory of an encounter I had with a friend earlier that week. She had suggested I hire a head hunter to find me a conventional 9-5 job with a 401K and the opportunity to climb the corporate ladder. Even my blank expression and unenthusiastic response didn't convince her that an important job title, a daily commute in heavy Denver area traffic, and a fancy office was not what I wanted. The entire concept might have appealed to me when I was much younger, but now just thinking about that lifestyle made me feel lightheaded and nauseous. My goals and priorities didn't align with this type of career paradigm any longer. I wanted to do something that would make a difference. Unfortunately, I couldn't think of a single job that was realistic, appealing, and soul confirming. I wondered what was wrong with me and who had stolen my motivation. Tears started to flow and quickly turned to gut deep sobs as I realized that my useful years on this earth were quickly disappearing. In the breaths between sobs, I thought I could hear the faint whinnies of many horses.

That night in my dreams, those horses came to me and delivered a gentle but urgent message. When I woke that morning, it bothered me that I couldn't remember what they had said. It wasn't until later in the day that I noticed a strong knowing emerging from somewhere deep inside of me. My purpose suddenly became clear—to share with equestrians the sacred space with horses where true communion is possible.

I had learned about the sacred space while living on my secluded ranch in northwestern Colorado. In the quiet isolation and beauty of the White River valley, my horses had taught me how to be more natural and connected to myself, the earth, and all animals. As I became more present, aware, and disconnected from technology, the sacred space emerged. In that space, I began to learn and understand the silent energy language of the earth and all life forms. At the time I didn't know HOW I was doing this, the ability just seemed to evolve on its own. In the sequestered environment of the ranch, communion with horses and other animals just happened—naturally.

When I moved to a small ranch about an hour from a major metropolitan area, it became apparent that people had fewer opportunities to learn to commune with animals—heart-to-heart and mind-to-mind—in the same way that my horses had taught me. There were equestrians who were open to learning my methods, but they seemed to believe that I possessed some special gift that was unattainable without years of spiritual study and practice. It was hard to convince them otherwise because what happens is silent and appears to work like magic.

For many mainstream equestrians, a strictly spiritual approach to teaching communion with a horse is neither appealing or believable. As a researcher, I became driven to discover how science might help explain the silent energy exchange that makes communion between and among species possible. In my search for a scientific explanation for the heart and mind connection that occurs between humans and horses, I realized that I couldn't totally ignore spiritual explanations—those things that science can't measure. Although books are generally classified as nonfiction (science) or fiction (spirit), in this case the division is not that clear. Only through the blending of science and spirit can we experience the sacred space.

As you read on, keep in mind that scientific validity is achieved in many different ways. To be scientific, something has to be quantifiable (measurable), objective, testable, predictable, and reproducible. Although I have made every attempt to provide a scientific explanation for all the topics presented in this book, there are a few instances where it is currently impossible to measure what is occurring given our current level of technology. In these instances, if I performed an action or applied a stimulus to many different horses—and observed a consistent reaction or predictable outcome—I formed a scientific theory. The aim of most scientific studies is to prove a theory wrong. I spent years experimenting and trying to prove the theories, principles and practices I present in this book don't work. But they do!

When I started writing down my thoughts and experiences with horses, I never dreamed they would eventually become a book. My initial goal was to create several short instruction manuals to hand out at my clinics. That all changed when I had the privilege of watching Frédéric Pignon and Magali Delgado at a unique and inspiring clinic in Colorado. (This husband and wife team are the creative force behind Cavalia, the incredible equestrian theater production that sells out to audiences around the world.) I watched in awe, mesmerized by the gentle, yet effective, impact they had on horses and people. It was incredibly profound. I extend my heart-felt appreciation to this astounding husband and wife team for inspiring me to be braver than I felt, and to share a new powerful paradigm with my fellow equestrians in the form of a book, clinics/symposiums, and private consultations.

In the following pages, I'll guide you through a process that, at this moment, you may not believe is possible. The process is easy, effective, and fun. This work truly is based on science, not magic. You'll be able to create changes and achieve results with your horses(s) in a predictable, repeatable, objective, and testable manner.

Happy experimenting!

Susan D. Fay, PhD

Throughout this book, an attempt was made to protect the identity and confidentiality of the horses and people whose experiences were documented in story form. While names and locations may have been changed, the events are factual.

Introduction

"That's one small step for (a) man, one giant leap for mankind."

—Neil Armstrong

In 1969, Neil Armstrong, Michael Collins, and Buzz Aldrin took off in Apollo 11. They had their sights set on the moon. At least 600 million people sat in front of their TVs captivated by Neil Armstrong as he took his first step into a new world.[1] He showed us that the impossible is possible when science is mixed with a giant dose of faith.

Humans like to travel to new places. They enjoy challenges and strive to find better ways to do things. As a result, new scientific discoveries happen every day. But science doesn't have all the answers. There are still things that science has a hard time explaining—that's where faith steps in.

In this book, I share another giant leap—for equestrians. I present scientific explanations for some of the unbelievable things that happen when people interact with horses. But you may have to take a few leaps of faith. Consider that some things we experience when interacting with horses defy scientific explanation. But just because some things can't be scientifically measured yet, it doesn't make them any less real.

Some equestrians experience the unexplainable on a regular basis. They may hesitate to tell anyone what happens to them for fear of ridicule. Perhaps, they share their experiences with a select few. There are a handful of equestrians who don't care what others think. They forge onward, unafraid. Still others have a gift that allows horses in their presence to do unbelievable things. These people may not think they do anything special. Maybe they assume it's normal and natural for amazing things to happen. As a result, they don't give much thought to what they are doing that makes their interactions with horses extraordinary.

For more than thirty years, I studied the horsemen and horsewomen who have *The Gift*. As a result, I discovered some of the things these people do that allow them to interact with horses in an easy and effortless way. My goal is to help you discover and unwrap this same type of natural gift with horses. When you take your newly developed gift with horses into the sacred space, unbelievable things begin to occur.

Perhaps you haven't found your gift because it's hiding behind a thick fog of limiting beliefs, scattered thoughts, and/or negative emotions. If this sounds like you, I'll give you ways to lift the fog that prevents you from seeing your gift. But activating the gift will take dedication, time, and effort. It's not a magic pill.

You may not yet believe that you are capable of going far beyond your current level of horsemanship. But if you open your mind and let fresh ideas flow in, you may discover unknown abilities within you. You must then decide whether you can take a leap of faith and let go of ideas about how things work and what is possible.

The amount of time and effort you put into discovering and cultivating your gift depends on you. I'm only able to show you where it is, help you unwrap it, and teach you how it operates. You must supply the energy and desire to make it work.

What is *The Gift*?

The Gift has many pieces to assemble before it operates at its greatest potential. These pieces include:

- The ability to control your thoughts and emotions.
- The capacity to understand yourself, inside and out.
- A desire to perceive the world from the horse's perspective. And then, to become more horse-like in your interactions with them.
- An eagerness to learn how to "speak" a universal language that both you and your horse understand.
- An awareness of the energy field and how to tap into it to create more positive and enjoyable experiences for you and your horse.
- The capacity to stay in the present moment, so you can BE with your horse.
- A commitment to slowing down—mentally, physically, and emotionally—when you're around horses.
- The passion to connect with another being—heart-to-heart and mind-to-mind.
- The ability to keep an open mind, loving heart, and joyous attitude in your interactions with horses.

I'll cover each of these pieces in much greater detail in the following chapters. You don't have to have all of these abilities in place before you begin to enjoy a better connection with your horse. But as you practice and become proficient at each skill, the interactions with your horse will start to become easier and more natural. You'll go from mere connection to communion.

As you can see, the things you do to uncover your gift with horses don't resemble a normal horse training method. That's because they're a people training method. They are what you can do to perceive and interact in this world more like a horse. If you commit to incorporating the principles in this book, I'm sure your horse will love the change in you!

There are no rules in this people training book. You'll find that as you notice your thoughts and emotions, you practice the exercises in each chapter, and you play with the energy field, your horse will reward you for your efforts. He or she will become calmer and more willing. Just give yourself time to learn and use these new concepts. Trying to rush this process can slow it down.

Don't worry—you won't have to throw out any of your current horse training methods or change your riding style. The concepts in this book are about making a shift in you. What you learn will enhance what you're currently doing with your horse.

As you practice the exercises in this book, you'll unearth abilities you didn't know you had. You never lost them. They just atrophied from lack of use. These aren't mystical abilities, and you don't need to download a special app to access them. You already have all the internal hardware and software needed to restore your lost senses and abilities and put them to use again. Once you do, get ready for the ride(s) of your life!

Your conversation with your horse will go from mere words (techniques) to true communion. The universal language you learn to speak with your horse is free of words, but rich in images, intentions, empathy, and energy. You'll develop your own inter-species translation device. It's one that already exists inside of you . . . you merely need to turn it back on!

If you're reading this book, you're probably someone who's not satisfied with staying in the same place. You may feel that something is missing from most of the current horse training techniques. If you have questioned the status quo, then you are someone who dreams of reaching new heights of understanding, not only for yourself, but for the sake of your equine partner.

The places you explore on this journey you're about to undertake may appear as illusive, remote, and unfamiliar as the moon once was to man. However strange it may seem, it's a place that was once natural to all humans. It's a place where you experience an increased awareness of yourself and the world around you.

Just like Neil Armstrong, you'll be able to see where you came from, while also stepping foot into a whole new world.

CHAPTER 1

The Revelation

"When you change the way you look at things, the things you look at change."

—Dr. Wayne Dyer

My whole body was shaking uncontrollably. Waves of fear and sorrow traveled down the lead rope I was holding in my trembling hand. At the end of rope stood a beautiful red gelding. My storm of emotions appeared to have no effect on him whatsoever. Peering into his beautiful soft brown eyes, it seemed that he was trying to calm me down—like I was the one with a problem. I wondered if he was in shock or just too tired to fight any longer. Or maybe he knew that he couldn't escape his fate . . . and he was waiting patiently for death to rescue him.

Trapped between the steel bars of the cattle guard, there was no way that three normal people could get him out—alive. My neighbor was on the way with his gun. We couldn't think of any other option.

Even though this nightmare scenario would soon come to an end, I knew the details would remain in my memory forever.

Some things are impossible to forget. Looking back now, I'm grateful for the precious gift this horse was about to give me . . .

Cattle guard

Note: A cattle guard is a metal grate placed over a depression. Ranchers use it when then want to drive between fenced areas without having to get out and open a gate. A cattle guard is placed along a roadway or entrance to a fenced pasture and acts as a visual and physical obstacle to livestock. The spacing between the pipes prevents animals from trying to walk across it. The guard is wide enough that most livestock won't try to jump over it.

THE RED GELDING

The day began when I was startled out of deep slumber by the neighs of hungry horses. It was late November and a layer of arctic air had settled over the White River Valley in northwestern Colorado. For more than a week the temperatures had stayed well below freezing. This day was no exception. After feeding the horses and hurriedly rushing through the ranch chores, I decided it was far too cold to exercise horses. The weather offered me the perfect excuse to grab a good book and curl up in front of the fireplace.

Around 4:00 in the afternoon, I looked up from my book as the realization hit me. I had to venture out into the cold to feed the horses and cows their evening meal. As I pulled on my boots and zipped up my heavy jacket, the thermometer caught my eye. "Geez," I thought to myself sarcastically, "It's a balmy −32° F!"

With my winter gear on, I took a deep breath and opened the door. It took a few moments for my body to adjust to the abrupt temperature change of nearly 100° F. My only thought was to finish my evening tasks as quickly as possible and return to the warmth of the fireplace.

Making my way to the barn, my breath created a dense fog in front of my face. My eyes watered from the sting of the frigid air and soon a thin layer of delicate ice coated my eyelashes. With each step, the sound of the crystalline snow squeaking beneath my boots interrupted the quiet stillness of the air. Unfortunately, the heavy boots and gloves I was wearing were proving defenseless against the intrusive cold. My fingers and toes felt like they were on fire inside—a painful and surreal sensation that happens when the blood flow to your extremities slows so that there is more available to keep your vital organs warm.

Approaching the barn, the first thing I spotted was the faint silhouettes of my horses. A thin white cloud camouflaged their features. Mist rose from their nostrils as they exhaled, like puffs of smoke from fire-breathing dragons.

Once at the barn, I tossed each horse extra hay and filled up their heated water tanks. Usually, I took my time doing the evening chores. The sound of horses munching hay and blowing softly through their noses in rhythmic sighs was like a comforting lullaby. But with darkness looming, I didn't linger. Soon the sun would retreat behind the mountain and any small bit of heat it had created during the day would dissipate into the clear night sky.

After a body-numbing hour in the cold, I was relieved to be done. But as soon as I stepped inside the welcome warmth of my house, the phone rang. "Hi Susie, It's Laura." She was having trouble getting the words out.

Her tone immediately put me on alert. I asked, "Is something wrong?"

"Yes!" she stuttered. "Hurry . . . one of your horses is trapped in the cattle guard at the end of your road."

Alarmed, I mumbled, "I'll be right out." My heart was pounding and I felt faint.

As I zipped up my coat, I pondered the fact that Laura and I didn't have the manpower, equipment, or strength to free the horse. The graphic stories of horses breaking their legs trying to escape from a cattle guard echoed in my mind.

As I ran toward the barn, my mind raced. Had I missed feeding one of my horses? No. Had I left a gate or stall door open? No. Why did one of my horses leave their hay, the other horses, and the comfort of the barn? It made no sense.

In a daze, I grabbed the closest halter and lead rope. I knew these two items would be useless in a rescue attempt. Their only real purpose was to calm my nerves.

Dread soon replaced my initial panic as I made my way down the road. Laura and I were on our own. Any additional help was hours away. Cell phones didn't work in the valley. They were like the halter and lead rope I desperately clung to. Useless.

When I neared the cattle guard, the blurred outline of a horse emerged out of the haze. Once my eyes adjusted to the approaching darkness, I recognized the muscular sorrel gelding. He belonged to my neighbor Ben. To my surprise, the horse was standing quietly, seemingly unaware of his predicament. Laura was stroking his neck, trying to comfort them both. We stood in silence for a moment, overcome by the hopelessness of the situation. I heard Laura mutter, "I will go get the owner. I'll make sure he brings his gun."

While I stood there waiting for Laura and Ben, a startling thought came into my mind. It might be possible to "talk" to the horse. "For Pete's sake," I mumbled to myself. "The cold must have affected my mind. I'm no Dr. Doolittle."

"Oh well," I reasoned. "No one will ever know. No harm in trying."

I'd heard that animals could read the pictures in our minds, but I was skeptical. An internal debate seemed pointless given the circumstances, so I started making pictures in my mind. In my imagination, I saw the horse navigating his way out of the cattle guard. Calmly.

If the horse could interpret my mind pictures, there was a small chance he could get out on his own. He had solid footing beneath him. The below zero temperatures and recent heavy snowfalls had formed a hard-packed base under the grate.

As I continued to send positive thoughts and images to the gelding, a strange sense of calm and warmth suddenly washed over me. I closed my eyes and encouraged the gelding—in my mind—to try. Then I gave the lead rope a gentle pull. To my astonishment, he moved forward a few feet just as I pictured. Then in one powerful movement, he lifted his front feet from the grate and launched himself out of the cattle guard. That one gigantic leap landed him on solid ground. He was out! Uninjured!

Laura and Ben appeared a few moments later. There was astonished silence. The humans spoke no words.

At first, I wasn't sure if the quivering in my body was a result of the cold, excess adrenalin, or something more profound. I watched Ben lead his horse down the road and they slowly disappeared into the mist. At the same time, I felt the fog of doubt begin to lift from my mind.

I turned toward my house, surprised at the clarity that seemed to increase with every step. I would never *see* my interactions with horses quite the same again. The big red gelding had just presented me the grandest gift—a glimpse into another realm. A chance introduction to the sacred space where the unbelievable happens.

I was transformed on a profound level. My paradigm had shifted and I could not go back to my old ways of thinking. I decided that how I trained and interacted with horses had to change. The gift from the red gelding was far too precious to ignore.

I began searching for a way to explain to myself, and others, what had happened that cold November evening. It wasn't long before my quest for answers turned into a full-blown expedition. I immersed myself in books and workshops on the subjects of equine behavior, psychology, hypnosis, Neurolinguistic Programming (NLP), quantum physics, spirituality, and energy work.

My long journey took me past the simple idea of interspecies communication. I went to places beyond my imagination. After my exhaustive quest, I arrived at two main conclusions:

> 1. Humans can communicate—on some level—with other species. They merely need to reawaken their dormant natural senses.
>
> And
>
> 2. True communion with another being—heart-to-heart and mind-to-mind—is the foundation for communication and understanding. It's a doorway to the sacred space.

You're invited to embark with me on an amazing adventure. Together we'll explore the places where true communion and communication happens. You'll discover how to create it in your relationships, whether they are human or equine. To pack for this journey, you only need three things:

A desire to learn

An open mind

A loving heart

CHAPTER 2

Getting on the Same Wavelength(s)

"While I was sleeping, I had a beautiful dream that all the people of the world got together on the same wavelength and began helping each other."

—Stevie Ray Vaughan

Have you ever had the feeling of being totally connected to someone? If so, you may have known what the other person was about to say, even before they said it. It wasn't necessary to explain to them—in words—your innermost emotions. They knew. And the amazing thing was that you understood them too. You could finish each other's thoughts or sentences. There was an easy flow—or an exhilarating excitement—to the encounter. Your time together left you both feeling recognized, accepted, and acknowledged.

When describing this experience to a friend, you may even have said, "It felt like the two of us were on the same wavelength." Wouldn't you love to say this about you and your horse?

If your answer is, "Yes!" keep reading. You'll soon learn a science-based process that allows you to create a silent energy

9

connection with other people—and your horse—whenever you want! You're actually doing it already, just unconsciously.

In this chapter, you'll begin to understand that the phrase, *being on the same wavelength,* is not just a figure of speech. Dr. Allen M. Schoen, DVM, suggests that there is an interactive and constantly changing energy field that surrounds us. In his Transpecies Field Theory, Dr. Schoen proposes that an energy field is produced when we connect and interact with another being, whether it's human or animal.[1] In other words, our behaviors create an energy field (i.e., energy waves) that affects others. And the energy field created by others affects us. This energy is generated, not through words, but through the energy emitted by our body as it reacts physiologically to our thoughts, intentions, and behaviors. Therefore, to learn how to get on the same wavelength with another being, you first need to understand the energy field.

The Energy Field

The energy field is made up of electromagnetic energy emitted by the earth and all living things.[2] While invisible to our eyes, energy fields aren't some imaginary thing that only exists in fairy tales or sci-fi movies.[3] Scientists have invented devices to measure energy fields that we can't detect using our human senses. (Or can we? More about that later.) Electrocardiograms (EKGs) measure the electrical energy created by the heart,[4] electroencephalograms (EEGs) measure the electrical energy created by the brain,[5] galvanic skin response (GSR) sensors measure the electrical resistance of the skin,[6] and magnetometers, or a simple compass, measures the earth's electromagnetic field.[7]

Our bodies pick up, and react to, electromagnetic energy from the field. We may not see or hear it, but we sense it (in our body).[8,9] Currently you may not consciously perceive changes in the electromagnetic energy field, but soon you'll learn how to increase your awareness of it. People who sense electromagnetic energy from the field (at a conscious level) have what we call a sixth sense. Unfortunately, these people are often considered crazy or eccentric. It's hard to prove this ability scientifically, but there is ample antidotal evidence.

Animal magnetism is a term used to describe the traits of someone who attracts admiring fans using some type of invisible force.[10] What a person with animal magnetism actually has is the ability to create a positive electromagnetic energy field around themselves. Their energy field is so strong that it affects everyone in their immediate proximity. They draw people to them because their energy makes others feel good.

> **Wouldn't it be wonderful if you could have animal magnetism around your horse?**

If your answer is, "Of course!" continue on. By the end of this chapter, you'll understand how. But first, it's important to know the ways you generate a positive electromagnetic field around your body.

You're actually doing it right now. Are you aware of your energy field? Do you know how it's affecting those around you?

If not, don't feel bad. Most of us were never taught that it is important to understand—or even pay attention to—our own energy field, or "energy signature."[11] Your energy signature is what your horse senses or "sees." People sense it too, but unconsciously—it's the first impression you make on them.

Your energy signature is like your written signature. It identifies who you are. But, unlike your written signature, it changes. Sometimes drastically. This is because your thoughts and emotions influence your energy signature. Your heart (emotions) and brain (thoughts) create electromagnetic energy. Just like your first and last name make up your written signature, your heart and brain make up your energy signature. Unless, you're meditating, comatose, or brain dead, your thoughts and emotions are constantly changing. Therefore, your energy signature is frequently changing as well.

The Three Human Brains

It may seem like the brain in our head is in charge of everything we think and feel. But it isn't. Scientists have discovered that we also have a brain in our heart and in our gut. These are considered brains because they have their own nervous systems that process information received from our senses. These two other brains can influence our thoughts and emotions. Unfortunately, our three brains don't always arrive at the same conclusions.[12] When you struggle making a decision, it may be because your three brains aren't in agreement!

Most of us only connect with our heart and gut brains on a subconscious level. We intuitively sense the existence of all three "brains." Otherwise, why would we commonly hear people say, "I had a gut feeling," "We had a heart-to-heart talk," or "I felt like the two of us were on the same wavelength . . . it was like we were reading each other's mind?"

All three brains receive information from the energy field. When one of your senses detects something in the environment, the nervous system (one or more of the three) turns this information into an electrical impulse, a chemical (i.e., hormone or neurotransmitter), a pressure wave, or electromagnetic field. The brain in your head then processes this information and decides what action it needs to take. If the action is a thought or emotion, electromagnetic energy is emitted from your body.[13]

As you receive and emit electromagnetic energy, you're having a conversation with the energy field. You're talking to everyone and everything around you. It's a silent, but important, conversation.

Horses naturally have energy conversations with each other and things in their environment. If you want to have a meaningful conversation with your horse, learn to connect with him or her through the energy field. You still communicate through your physical aids (e.g., seat, legs, hands, voice, and weight). But when you communicate through the energy field as well, the conversation becomes deeper and more meaningful to the horse.

It's not that difficult to communicate with your horse through the energy field. You already are, just at a subconscious level. All you need to do to bring the conversation to a conscious level is: 1) Hone your senses; 2) Pay attention to messages from your senses; and 3) Gain control over your energy signature (i.e., thoughts and emotions). When you do, you will turn on your interspecies communication and translation device.

A conversation requires a vocabulary and listening skills. You "listen" to the energy field through messages from your three brains. You talk through your thoughts and emotions. Both of these create the "words" that your horse sees and hears.

In the following section, you'll discover how each of your three brains communicate. Energetically, that is. As you learn about the different brains, try to imagine times when you heard your gut, heart, or the brain in your head try to communicate something important. Did you listen?

The Gut Brain

Of the three brains, the gut is the most basic or primitive. Its job is to warn you of impending danger, or to steer you in the right direction.[14] You probably can't count the number of times you heard someone say, "I had a gut feeling I shouldn't have done that, but I ignored it. I wished I would have listened."

The gut receives information from the energy field, but its focus is on keeping you safe. If it feels a physical or emotional threat, it sends that information up to the logical brain in your head for processing.[15] When you become more open to what that "funny" feeling in the pit of your stomach is trying to say, you might be more inclined to listen. It's sensing something that you aren't consciously aware of. You can strengthen this sense every time you pay attention to it and honor its message.

Because the gut brain is basic, it provides simple yes or no type answers. The yes or no answer is related to a feeling or an intuition. If you get an uncomfortable feeling or negative emotion comes up when you are considering doing something, chances are your gut is trying to tell you to stop and reconsider.

The Gut Brain and Horses

Let's say Jen's in a hurry to get a ride in after work. She notices that her horse is acting jittery and doesn't want to stand still to get brushed and saddled. Her mind is not on her horse or riding. Instead, she's going over the awful encounter she had with a coworker that afternoon. It made her feel so angry. Not only that, she can't stop thinking about all the things she needs to get done at work the next day.

Jen keeps ignoring the nagging feeling in her stomach. She can't put her finger on what it is, so she ignores the sensation and gets on her horse. She immediately per-forms a new aerial stunt—but she didn't perfect the land yet. Thump!

If Jen had been listening to her gut, the situation might have turned out dif-ferently. This time, even though she was in a hurry and had a lot of things on her mind, she stopped to notice that her horse was acting anxious. She slowed down and become quiet. She didn't ignore the strange feeling in her gut—she listened to it. Somehow, she knew that something bad might happen if she continued.

She checked her horse for any sore areas and carefully examined her tack. Then she checked in with herself. That's when she realized how anxious and unfocused **she** was. Jen took a deep breath and quieted her mind. She let go  of her anger toward her coworker. She realized that he was also worried about the looming project deadline. Jen closed her eyes and took some deep breaths. Her horse took a big breath and let out a huge sigh. The bad feeling lifted. Jen got on her horse and the ride went well.

If you've ignored your gut feelings for a long time, it may take some time before you learn the difference between when it is telling you "yes," and when the answer is "no." The key to getting clear answers is to stop, quiet your mind, close your eyes, breathe deeply, bring your energy down, and focus your attention on your stomach. Dread or a feeling of danger are telling you to stop and reconsider what you're doing.

The Heart Brain

The heart is the "brain" that receives **emotional** information from the energy field.[16] But that's not all. When you create an emotion, your heart converts it to electromagnetic energy and sends it into the field. Your heart's energy waves communicate your emotional state to others.[17] If you're listening (with your heart), you pick up their emotional state as well.

For more than twenty years, scientists at the HeartMath Institute (HMI) have studied the electromagnetic energy created and emitted by the heart. They discovered that the heart is the first organ in the body to sense emotional information from the body or from someone or something in the energy field. This information is processed by the heart's nervous system and then the information is sent on to the (main) brain for further analysis.[18]

Scientists use a device called a magnetometer to measure the electromagnetic energy emitted by the heart. The magnetometer detects the energy and displays it on a graph.[19] Using this device, scientists at HMI found that a human's heart energy can be detected up to 10 feet away from their body.[20] The electromagnetic energy emitted by the human heart is also much greater in amplitude (stronger) than that emitted by the brain. Sixty times larger![21] And, a horse's heart energy is five times stronger than a human's![22]

Thoughts and emotions affect the heart's electromagnetic wave pattern. Positive thoughts and emotions create an energy wave pattern that is very smooth and regular. When this happens, the heart's rhythm is considered by scientists to be "coherent." Negative thoughts and emotions create an irregular heart rhythm and low coherence.[23]

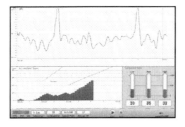 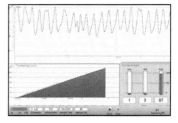

Low Coherence (Stressed)   High Coherence (Relaxed)

Figure 1: Low and High Heart Coherence

When your heart is in high coherence, your mind, emotions, and heart are in alignment. This is a state of health that increases your intuition and creativity and allows you to more easily access to your inner guidance and your ability to connect with others. When you maintain high heart coherence, your blood pressure lowers, your stress levels drop, and you feel calm and relaxed. You feel good because your "main" brain released mood-enhancing beta-endorphins (a natural pain reliever).[24] In this

state, all of your body's systems are working together and operating at an optimal level.[25]

On the other hand, negative thoughts and emotions create a
chaotic and irregular heart wave rhythm. This, in turn, negatively affects your respiration and blood pressure rhythms.
When your body's systems are affected by low heart coherence,
your brain's ability to process information, solve problems, and
be creative is reduced.[26]

Because the heart's energy field is so large, it easily picks up
electromagnetic information from the energy field, or sends it
out into the energy field.[27] Every time your emotions change,
there is a change in the electromagnetic field emitted by your
heart. Because the heart's energy field extends outside your
body, anyone near you will be affected by this change in energy.

The dominate (i.e., higher amplitude or stronger) wave in the
energy field will cause other surrounding waves to synchronize
(i.e., copy or entrain) with it.[28] Consider the implications of this
the next time you're having negative emotions. You're creating a
negative energy field around your body. This negative field can
affect your horse and those around you—and possibly cause
them to be negative too!

Start experimenting with creating a high heart coherence.
You'll know that you're successful if you start to feel relaxed and
in a good mood. To learn how to train your heart rhythm, you
can purchase a device called an emWave.[29] You connect the
emWave to your ear lobe and plug it into your phone or computer. The device then displays your heart rhythm on the screen.
(See Figure 1.) The program will guide you through breathing
exercises and games that will help you increase your heart coherence.

If you use an emWave regularly, you'll begin to learn how
you feel when your heart is in high coherence due to positive
thoughts and emotions and when it is in low coherence due to
negative emotions, stress, or anxiety.

Heart Energy and Horses

Equestrians who know about the power of heart energy can use it in two different ways:

1. Create their own positive heart wave and send it to the horse.

   or

2. Spend time in the horse's energy field and absorb (entrain) to his heart wave pattern.

Many people want to have a deeper and more meaningful connection with their horse. This happens when heart wave patterns synchronize between two or more beings. Horses and people like to be around someone whose heart rhythm is in high coherence. It makes them feel good too! When two or more beings are in high heart coherence, they connect on a deep emotional level. In that place, they feel each other's emotions.[30]

When I work with equestrians, I help them access the power of heart coherence to develop a communion with their horse. At one of my clinics, a participant named Linda told me that although her horse would do what she asked, he was always hesitant to join up with her in the round pen. However, once caught, he was obedient and did what she asked.

As I approached them for our session, I noticed they were both in the round pen together—but not. She was sitting on a box in the middle. Her horse was along the fence, looking out toward the other horses.

Walking down the hill toward the round pen, I made sure I was in high heart coherence. As I neared the round pen, Linda's horse looked at me and walked over. He followed me around the round pen to the entrance. Linda was astonished. We proceeded to talk about heart energy and positive emotions. That's all. A week later she called me back, ecstatic. She told me that she had been practicing the principles I taught her, and her horse had made great progress in just seven days. She felt that he was now asking to be around her and seemed to seek out her company.

When working with Linda, I first had her recall a time when she had felt very connected to her horse. She closed her eyes and imaged the thoughts and emotions that she experienced during that time. Then, Linda focused on breathing that positive emotion through her heart and creating an imaginary bubble of positive heart energy around her body. She relaxed her mind and let the images float through her thoughts. Her horse responded positively to her new energy and became easier to catch and more willing to do what she asked.

Do this same exercise if you want to create a positive thought or emotion. The thought or situation you recall doesn't necessarily need to be related to horses. It's only important that you imagine a time when you had a positive emotion. Imagining a time when you were happy, joyful, grateful, or content puts your heart into high coherence.

> **But what if you're having a really bad day and it's hard for you to create a positive emotion?**

The second way to accomplish high heart coherence is to be in the presence of a calm and relaxed horse. You don't need to be touching the horse, just sit or stand near him or her. Imagine your heart and mind merging with the horse's relaxed energy.

Close your eyes and try to create a feeling of gratitude, love, or other positive emotion in your body. Think of a time or a situation when you felt this positive emotion. Imagine that you're letting go of any negative thoughts and emotions. You may even do this while mucking a stall or brushing the horse. The repetitive motion in your body will also help you become calmer so that you can entrain to the horse's heart wave pattern.

Just note that **some**, but not all, horses can help you become calmer. Choosing a horse who is confident and emotionally stable will make this process easy because he naturally produces a more coherent heart wave pattern for you to entrain to. Putting an anxious person around an anxious horse can often make matters worse—for both parties. This situation can quickly become dangerous, so having a good read of the horse's emotional and mental state is vital. Either the human or the horse has to have high heart coherence to begin with, or this exercise doesn't work.

Horses have a remarkable ability to heal us with their heart energy. This may be why they make such good "therapists." We often hear stories of how a horse helped someone through a difficult time. This happened because there was a true heart-to-heart connection between the horse and the human.

The Main Brain

Like the heart, the brain's energy field is not static. It changes based on what you think, the emotions you have, and your level of consciousness (i.e., wide awake, alert, drowsy, asleep).[31] Although the electrical energy produced by the brain is not as strong as the heart's, it still communicates with the energy field. Like the heart, the brain produces waves of electrical energy that fluctuate depending on what you're thinking or doing. Other people and animals can entrain to your brain's energy wave patterns just as they do to your heart's energy waves.[32]

In general, the more relaxed you are, the slower your brain waves. Anxiety, fear, worrying, over-thinking, and analyzing will cause your brain waves to become faster.[33]

This is important to remember when riding or interacting with a horse. If you get anxious, but have a calm and steady horse, you may entrain to his brain waves. However, if you're anxious, your horse may entrain to your rapid brain waves and become spooky, unfocused, and/or flighty. You're signaling to him that danger could be imminent and energetically communicating that he should be on the alert, ready to flee at any moment.

You can learn to feel when you're in a particular brain wave pattern. It's not hard, but it takes some practice and awareness. Your body or your mind will tell you. For example, if you have a headache, scattered/racing thoughts, inability to focus, and/or anxiety, it might be a good indication that your brainwaves are too fast and you need to close your eyes and breathe deeply to slow them down.[34] In the next sections, you'll learn the characteristics associated with different brain wave patterns. Once you do, you'll be able to recognize when you're in an optimal state of mind for interacting with horses.

> **Note:**
> If you're not a fan of science, just scan through this next section. But pay attention to the information on Beta and Alpha brain waves. These are the main ones you need to be familiar with when interacting with horses. Theta and Delta are primarily associated with deep relaxation and sleep. You probably don't want to be riding while your brain is trying to sleep!
>
> You can also come back to this next section if you need some clarification. For those of you who are science geeks, this next section may be too general. But, for our purposes, we only need a general understanding of brain waves. If you need more detailed information, there are entire books and other resources available on this subject.

The Science of Brain Waves

Neurons are cells in the brain that carry electrical impulses. You brain has a complex network of neurons that communicate with each other.[35] When sensory information reaches the brain, neurons are stimulated. The neuron creates an electrical impulse (i.e., action potential). The electrical signal causes the neuron to release a chemical neurotransmitter. Just as the name implies, the neurotransmitter can transfer information from one neuron to another. Whenever you do something, think something, sense something, or feel something (emotionally or physically), it causes neurons in one or more areas of your brain to fire (i.e., send electrical impulses and release a neurotransmitter).[36]

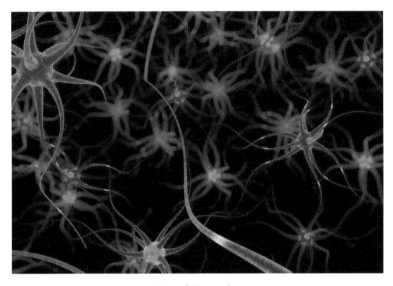

Neural Network

Be grateful for the neurons in your brain—they allow you to go about your daily activities without much conscious thought. You created a neural connection—or pathway—between neurons each time you learned something new. If you kept doing that same activity the same way, the neural pathway became stronger and faster.[37] Think of that neural pathway transforming from a dirt road to a paved super highway.

This process of strengthening the connection between neurons is called myelination.[38] Myelination allows you to do an activity quickly and easily without conscious thought. You have created many neural pathways—turned superhighways—in your brain. You may have them for activities such as driving, riding your horse, talking, walking, dancing, etc. When you can perform a maneuver or do something without having to think about the steps, you have a developed a neural superhighway for that activity.

The adult human has around 86 billion neurons. Every time a neuron fires, it connects to 1000 other neurons.[39] This creates a lot of electrical activity in your head!

Scientists use an electroencephalograph (EEG) to measure the brain's electrical activity. Through a series of sensors placed at specific locations on the scalp, the EEG detects the brain's electrical activity. Each sensor monitors the electrical activity in a particular region of the brain.[40]

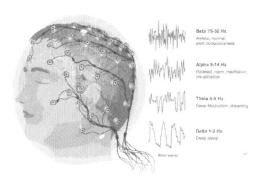

Electroencephalograph (EEG)

The power or amplitude of a brain wave is measured in microvolts. The height of the wave (on the computer output) corresponds to the amplitude. The number of wave cycles per second is the frequency of the brain wave. The frequency is measured in hertz (HZ).[41]

There are five main categories of brain waves. The category is based on a range of frequencies (HZ) that correspond to a state of consciousness—from wide awake and alert to deep sleep.

Your brain usually produces a combination of different frequencies of brain waves at any one time. They are constantly changing, depending on what you're doing or thinking and your emotional state.[42] Remember that others, including your horse, can entrain to your brain wave pattern, or you to theirs.

The following pages contain lists of the main characteristics associated with each brain wave category.[43] These are generalizations, so use this information as a guide. Interpreting actual brain wave patterns from an EEG is complicated and should be left up to a professional.

Most of us don't have access to an EEG or neurofeedback machine to give us information about our brain waves. But you can notice how you **feel** (emotionally and/or physically) when you produce a predominance of a particular type of brainwave. And you can begin to notice how your horse acts or reacts to changes in your brain wave pattern.

Categories of Brain Waves

Gamma (38–100 Hz)

Activities/Characteristics:

Heightened compassion
Universal love
Expanded consciousness
Surfacing of repressed or unpleasant memories and/or emotions
Whole brain activation
High-level information processing
Insights/intuition

Sensations/Feelings of Gamma:

Feeling of deep relaxation
Amplified senses
Increased awareness of surroundings
Hyper awareness of your body
Improved ability to focus and remember
Contentment
A deep knowing
Feeling of being in The Zone (Performing at a high level without need for conscious thought.)
Sensation of time distortion

Note: Only a limited amount of study has been conducted on this brain wave. Long-time meditators can produce Gamma. It is believed that people produce bursts of Gamma.

Beta (12–38 Hz)

Scientists have divided Beta into three categories: Beta1 (12–15 Hz), Beta2 (15–22 Hz) and Beta3 (22–38 Hz).

Activities/Characteristics of Beta1:

> Relaxed mind and body
> Gentle thinking

Activities/Characteristics of Beta2:

> Increased ability to focus and pay attention
> Enhanced problem solving and analysis skills
> Ability to think logically and make good decisions
> Boost in math, reading, and writing abilities

Sensations/Feelings of Beta1 or Beta2:

> Alert mind and body
> Focused
> Excited
> Happy

Activities/Characteristics of Beta3:

> Ability to solve complex problems
> Greater analysis and judgment skills
> Increased learning and integration of new information
> Heightened worry and anxiety
> Racing thoughts
> Over analysis

Sensations/Feelings of Beta3

> Euphoria
> Mania

Racing heart
Anxiety
Rapid breathing
Inability to concentrate
Headache
Blurry vision

Note: You may feel good in Beta3 because it seems like you get a lot done. But your brain and body become fatigued trying to maintain this brainwave pattern for extended periods. You will eventually experience a crash.

Alpha (8–12 Hz)

Activities/Characteristics:

Physically and mentally relaxed
Mind-body integration
Less focused on the outside world
Receptive mind
Enhanced learning and memory
Daydreaming, mental imagery
Light hypnosis
Heightened intuition and creativity

Sensations/Feeling of Alpha:

Relaxed body and mind
Lightly focused
Dreamy
Creative
Intuitive

Note: Notice how you feel when you're engrossed in a good book or movie or a creative project. You're probably producing a predominance of Alpha brain waves. In the lower range of Alpha, your intuition increases.

Theta (3–8 Hz)

Activities/Characteristics:

Deep hypnosis
Deep meditation
Spiritual insight
Increased intuition
Access to information not available to the conscious mind
Enhanced healing
Inner focus (no awareness of outside world)

Sensations/Feelings of Theta:

This is the state between consciousness and sleep. You experience Theta right before you fall asleep and while you dream. You produce Theta during dreaming sleep (REM).

Note: Some experienced meditators can remain conscious of their surroundings and what is happening around them while in Theta. It is also the place where memories of fear or unpleasant experiences reside.

Delta (.5–3 Hz)

Activities/Characteristics:

Sending and receiving messages on a subconscious level
Deep, dreamless sleep

Deep meditation

Empathy

Healing and regeneration of mind and body

Restorative sleep

Sensations/Feelings of Delta:

Loss of body awareness

Loss of conscious awareness

Note: People who are highly intuitive may produce some delta brain waves in an awake state. They can even have out-of-body experiences while in Delta.

Brain Waves and Horses

Of all the brain wave patterns, Beta1 and Alpha are those you should strive to produce when interacting with horses. Just like heart waves, you can change your brain waves by changing your thoughts and emotions. If you feel you're in Beta2 or Beta3, close your eyes and focus on taking several deep breaths. This will help you immediately produce more Beta1 or Alpha brain waves.

Talented horse/rider teams often fall under the influence of negative heart and brain waves. When this happens, they can't perform at their highest potential. In some cases, the rider or trainer recognizes that there is some kind of block in the horse's progress or problem with communication, but they didn't know how to fix it. The problem could be as simple as the horse spooking in the same corner of the arena, or as complex as getting consistent flying lead changes. The fix can often be as easy as changing the rider's heart and/or brain waves. (More about how to do this later!)

Equestrians often share with me that they wish they could have a sustainable or consistent connection with their horse.

They tell me they have tried different riding and groundwork techniques; they've attended training and behavioral seminars; they read countless books on the subject; and they've taken lessons from different equestrian masters. The new information or technique they learned worked for a while, but there was usually an inevitable return of the old problem or issue.

Now you know that there is a state of heart and mind that deepens connection, enhances communication, and decreases stress or anxiety. You understand that positive thoughts and emotions coupled with a slow Alpha brain wave pattern puts you in an optimum state to send and receive data from the energy field. Armed with this new information, you may feel a twinge of excitement when you imagine the implications for you and your horse. Hearts and minds speak a universal language when they unite on the same wavelength. When they do, communion is possible.

You may notice that I haven't advocated any particular horse training method or discipline. That's because brain and heart waves don't care what type of horse you have or the discipline you ride. And remember, this is a people training book! Everything you learn will make what you currently do with your horse better.

PAUL AND SAMMY—JOHN AND FLICKER

My friend Paul had attended some of my clinics, so he knew the importance of heart energy and he paid attention to his brain waves when interacting with his horse Sammy. Because he understood how to have an energetic conversation with her, they enjoyed a great working relationship. He loved to rope steers and so did Sammy—they seemed to bring out the best in each other. The guys Paul roped with on the weekends took great pride in their lack of emotional connection with their horses. They considered themselves tough competitors and real men.

Stan, one of the guys Paul roped with, was quick to correct his horse Charger for any small sign of disobedience. He jerked the reins and dug his spurs into the gelding's flanks any time he decided Charger wasn't listening or reacting fast enough. Stan insisted that he was turning his horse into a cow chasing machine by teaching him to obey immediately and without question. Paul noticed that Charger often acted just like a machine—a bucking machine, or one that broke down a lot because Stan didn't check the oil and ignored the funny noise under the hood.

Paul didn't let on to any of his roping buddies, but he deeply loved Sammy. One time at a competition, a girl (me) caught him kissing her on the nose. The girl just smiled. It was their little secret.

Paul and Sammy

Paul's horse was like a well-oiled machine with a heart. She never quit on him. Once when she tripped chasing a steer, Paul fell off. Sammy stopped and waited for him to get back in the saddle. At the end of the year, they won money, a buckle, a saddle, and a horse trailer.

Paul got it. John, the rider in the next story didn't. John had a very stressful job and riding was his "relaxation." But he couldn't relax his mind when he rode.

John's horse Flicker would do anything for him, but she was very sensitive. John showed Flicker in dressage. He would come home from work each night and ride her for about an hour. Watching them in the arena, I immediately knew John's mood. After a bad day at work, Flicker would perform at supersonic speed. She did every maneuver correctly, just really, really fast. One time when I filmed their session, John thought I was running the video in double speed. That's how fast!

On one of "Flicker's" bad days, John stopped and asked me how to slow her down. I told him to relax and make clear pictures of what he wanted her to do and then gently apply his aids to slow her. And, I added, he needed to make sure he projected good thoughts and positive emotions.

By the disgusted look on his face, it was clear that wasn't the answer John was looking for. He told me he was logical and didn't buy into that "voodoo" and emotional mumbo jumbo. He needed to know a stronger aid to use. I shrugged and told him I couldn't help him. After our brief conversation, John rolled his eyes at me and the two sped off together.

The Right and Left Brain

We often refer to people as being right or left brain. In reality, everyone uses both sides, or hemispheres, of their brain. Both sides work together at the same time. The brain's two hemispheres communicate with each other through a band of nerve fibers called the corpus callosum.[44]

When we think of someone as right or left brained, we're really evaluating them on the efficiency and speed of their neural connections (neural superhighway) and their state of consciousness (dominate brain wave pattern). For example, some people have a math superhighway inside their brain and they stay in Beta2 or Beta3 when solving math problems. For others, math lies at the end of a dirt path. They don't use that path often, so it's unfamiliar and difficult to navigate—or they try to solve math problems while in an Alpha brain wave pattern. Those people who have a complex superhighway system for a variety of tasks have taught their brain to think and organize information so that their routes are fast and efficient. They also know what state of consciousness is optimum for the task at hand—their desired destination. If you're interested in learning more about how you can develop this type of brain, read *The Organized Mind* by Daniel J. Levitin.[45]

Not all researchers believe that people are predominately right or left brained. In 2013, a group of neuroscientists challenged this common idea and declared that right or left-brain dominance is a myth.[46] Keeping that in mind, for our purposes it's helpful to use these terms as a way to understand how someone's mental superhighway system works, what routes they prefer to take, and what brain wave state they're currently in. Do they prefer to travel the logical and analytical route, or do they want to go down the scenic road leading to intuition and artistic expression? Remember, logic and analysis are the forte of high Beta brain waves; intuition and feel are more accessible when the brain waves slow down to low Beta and Alpha.

In general, people who we call right-brain dominate like to do things that require imagination, big picture thinking, emotions, creativity, artistry, daydreaming, and intuition.[47] Right-brain dominant people prefer horse training methods centered on feelings, intuition, and understanding the inner horse.

People who we call left-brain dominate like logic, words, analysis, linear thinking, math, methods, and facts.[48] Left-brain dominate people prefer horse training methods that are systematic, technique-based, and logical.

The ideal situation is to teach yourself what side of the brain is best for completing the task at hand and then adjust the brain wave pattern accordingly. The key is to learn how to switch back and forth easily. For example, trying to use your left brain's analytical abilities and high Beta brain waves to develop a systematic method to achieve intuition or better feel doesn't work well. As you know, intuition increases when brain waves slow down to Beta1 or Alpha. (Intuition can also increase in Gamma, but that brain wave pattern is often difficult for some people to achieve on a regular or sustained basis.)

Each hemisphere of your brain has its special talents, so don't decide to shut one or the other off. We have two sides of our brain for a reason—it gives us balance. There are books, Internet articles, apps, and training seminars available that can help you develop and integrate your right and left brain so you can become "double dominate." [49] When both sides work together, you have whole brain communication, which is the optimal way to use your brain.

One of the best examples of a double dominate person who used his right- and left-brain talents to the fullest was Leonardo da Vinci. He was an artist and a scientific genius. He used science as a foundation for his art, and his creativity and imagination as a catalyst for his scientific inventions. Because de Vinci was so good at using both hemispheres of his brain, he was able to engineer plans for a bicycle, airplane, submarine, and helicopter centuries before they were "re-invented," **and** create artistic masterpieces such as "The Last Supper" and the "Mona Lisa."[50]

Right- and Left-Brain People and Horses

Horses live in the realm of visual cues, intuition, emotions, and bodily feelings. A right-brain person understands this world. However, right-brain dominant people can run into problems with horses if they are too emotional or can't focus on details. They may need to add a dash of left-brain logic and organization. Highly left-brain people tend to make their interactions with horses very mechanical and systematic. They could benefit from a dash of right-brain intuition and feel.

There are some equestrians who evaluate a horse (or person) to determine if it's right- or left-brain dominate and if it displays characteristics of introversion or extroversion. First, these labels tend to put the person or horse into a box. Once inside the box, the label becomes attached to everything that person or horse does. People treat them like the label rather than as an individual. This is called *attribution bias* in psychology.[51]

Bernard Weiner, the researcher who developed Attribution Theory,[52] explains attribution bias as a phenomenon whereby people tend to make explanations for another person's (or animals) behaviors based on the outward things they observe, rather than taking into account the situation or the environment in which the behavior happens.[53]

Attribution bias can lead to a Fundamental Attribution Error.[54] This is the inability for a person to "see" or notice anything that doesn't fit within the label or belief they assigned to someone or something. In other words, they can only see the things that confirm the assigned label.[55] (You may have also noticed that people tend to ignore those things that don't confirm what they expect to see or hear. This is called perceptual, or inattentional blindness.[56]) Eventually, the person or animal will tend to act in accordance with the label, further confirming how "accurate" it is.

Labels are rigid. They don't take into account that an animal or person might behave differently in different situations. For most people and animals, extroversion and introversion, and right- and left-brain processing exist on a continuum. Let's look at a real-life example.

SANDRA AND RENEGADE

Sandra got a new horse that had been in a physically abusive situation. She named him Renegade Sandra was dedicated to taking her time to gain Renegade's trust. She was resolved to starting him over again . . . slowly and gently.

Sandra decided that the first thing she would do is observe how Renegade acted around her and try to determine his underlying personality traits. After a few days, she decided that based on his behaviors, he was a right-brain introvert. He was fearful and hesitant to do much. He also didn't seem to care for interaction of any type.

Now, armed with a label for Renegade, she felt confident that she knew how to proceed with his rehabilitation and training. She also knew what behaviors to expect from him.

But Sandra had just taken her first step toward committing a Fundamental Attribution Error leading to perceptual blindness. Instead of using her intuition, she stayed in her left brain, analyzing and studying each of Renegade's behaviors and reactions. She was quite proud of her ability to accurately label him.

What Sandra forgot to take into account was that Renegade might change after he became accustomed to his new surrounds, had better nutrition, and became more comfortable with her. One day, treating him as a right-brain introvert, he suddenly made a 180° and changed into a left-brain extrovert.

As she led him to the round pen, he seemed surer of himself. That made her happy. She continued to treat him gently, cautiously moving around him, trying not to spook or frighten him. But on this day, when she pushed him for a little more speed on his circles, he turned and lunged toward her. She barely moved to the side quick enough to avoid his charge. She rattled the plastic bag she had attached to a long stick to keep him from charging again. Unlike before, it didn't scare him and he ran past her at full speed. Renegade, it seemed, had turned into his name.

If Sandra had been using her right-brain intuition instead of the left-brain label, she may have seen the warning signs. She may have been more observant of Renegade's increasing confidence. She would have been able to read the signs, rather than letting the label define what she could "see."

Horses can often act one way around humans, and a completely different way around other horses, other people, or in different situations. While it's important to know about horse personality traits, don't let them lull you into thinking that's all that matters. In fact, staying in left-brain analytical thinking (e.g., labels, personality traits, training methods) can cause perceptual blindness and keep your intuition at bay. You need to rely more on intuition and your senses—especially common sense—when interacting with horses.

There is a more detailed discussion about horse labels in Chapter 7. For now, just keep in mind that labels should be interpreted with caution. Use labels as **guidelines**, rather than strict rules. Always keep in mind that labels are situational—they don't always apply when the situation changes.

The purpose of this chapter was to provide a research base for the concepts presented throughout the remainder of this book. You don't need to study and remember the details of how the energy field works—just know that it serves as the validation you need to conduct your own experiments. In each chapter, you'll learn some easy and practical ways to apply your invisible powers.

The true stories contained within the pages of this book are about normal people and their horses having extraordinary experiences. If you decide to embark down the road toward unlocking your gift, keep in mind that change doesn't materialize without some effort. Just like weight training, you need to invest time in building your energetic muscles.

CHAPTER 3

The Thought-Full and Emotional Human

"Rather than being your thoughts and emotions, be the awareness behind them."

—Ekhart Tolle, *A New Earth*

M ary sat cross-legged on the cold Yoga mat. She had hoped that the class would give her a moment of relief from the never-ending barrage of worrisome thoughts running through her mind. But she couldn't make them stop. She felt even more irritated when she heard the instructor's calm voice tell everyone to let go and empty their minds. Anger flushed over her face as she muttered under her breath, "That's easy for him to say, he's not living my life." The harder Mary tried to push her thoughts away, the more they pushed back, inundating her mind. She felt like a failure. She peeked through one eye and gazed around the room full of meditators. They all seemed serene and quiet. That made her even more frustrated. But Mary didn't realize she was on the precipice of a breakthrough . . . courtesy of her horse Max.

On the way to the stable after the meditation class, Mary decided that her scheduled riding lesson on Max would be a terrible idea, especially given her present state of mind. She needed someone to understand the pressures and disappointments of her life, not an instructor focused on pointing out all her riding faults. She worked hard to hide her flaws from people.

When Mary entered Max's stall, he softly nickered to her. His gentle gesture caused her dam of built up emotions to break. She buried her face in Max's soft neck, and her flood of tears soaked his beautiful ebony and white hair.

Mary and Max

She spoke to him about the negative thoughts that consumed her. He listened like the most empathetic therapist. She thought her negative thoughts and emotions would cause him to want to flee. Instead he stood patiently, waiting until she had confessed all of her inner conflicts, secrets, and insecurities. It was cathartic.

Her worries floated away and she took a deep breath. Max lowered his head, yawned, and chewed. He was more relaxed than she had ever seen him. She saddled him up and they had wonderful ride. Instead of spooking at imaginary things like he commonly did, he was focused and steady.

Mary called me immediately after her lesson, eager to find an answer for Max's curious response to her emotional release. She explained to me that after spilling her heart out, Max changed. I asked her if she was the one who changed and she seemed confused. After thinking it over for a moment, she excitedly blurted out, "It's the first time in my life I wasn't pretending to be someone I wasn't . . . I became congruent!" Mary realized being congruent—the same person inside and out—is why Max let down his defenses and relaxed. Before I could ask, she added, "You won't believe it . . . I was finally able to stop the self-criticism and endless mind chatter in my head!"

Thoughts

Our conscious minds are never quiet. Thoughts flow in and out of our awareness like an endless wave hitting the beach. If we're anxious, fearful, or worried, our thoughts can become like a Tsunami, engulfing our mind and drowning us in negativity. When this happens, our rational mind just stops working. We become overwhelmed and ineffective. Negative thought patterns can become habitual. If a person struggles with this problem on a regular basis, it can damage his or her relationships, both human and equine.

Thought Tsunamis can take over riders' minds. Often the rider can't figure out what to do to escape the destructive waves of thoughts. At a minimum, a horse may become agitated or anxious when the rider's thoughts are out of control. Sometimes riders end up on the ground, or clinging for dear life on a runaway horse. An experience like this is traumatizing for both the horse and the rider.

A rider who is able to calm his or her own mind is much more effective in calming the horse than a rider who punishes the horse for his natural reaction to the human's stressful energy. Our thoughts profoundly affect our horses and Thought Tsunamis are preventable. Therefore, it's important to become aware of how your horse reacts to your thoughts. Some horses are better than others at weathering a rider's thought storms.

Unless you're someone who spends a lot of time meditating, you may not be aware of your habitual thoughts. That's because thoughts tend to grab and hold your attention only if they're dramatic—really good or really bad. Otherwise, they enter your awareness and fade back out, only to be replaced by yet another one. Thoughts don't like to be held back, so any moment of silence provides the perfect opportunity for the next wave of thoughts to roll on in.

The goal of most meditative practices is to reach a state of "no mind" or "no thought."[1,2] When you're in a quiet meditative state, it takes a lot of practice before you can have a thought enter your mind and be able to release it immediately. Like a little puppy chasing a ball, your mind likes to follow your thoughts. They're definitely more fun and interesting than nothing!

When asked if they meditate, most equestrians tell me they don't have the time. There is often a twinge of guilt in their voice, like they're about to get scolded. I understand that for most people, the demands of everyday life make it difficult to find a quiet place to sit and do nothing. There are much more productive ways to spend a few precious moments of free time. Most equestrians would do anything for an extra hour each day with their horse.

> **If I propose a guilt-free alternative to traditional meditation that would fit into your busy schedule, would you be willing to give it a try?**

Would the offer sound even better if you knew that you didn't have to carve out a special time and place to practice it?

But wait, there's more to this offer. Would you be interested if it helped you develop greater focus, connection, and creativity? What about if you could use it to control those pesky negative thoughts and emotions that often arrive uninvited? Would you give it a shot? The best part of this offer is that you don't have to buy anything—except this book!

For lack of a better marketing term, I call my offer "Productive Contemplation," or PC for short. Just like the word implies, PC is results oriented. Now, if someone asks, you can say, "My meditative practice is PC." How could anyone shame you for being PC!

Practicing PC may take some effort on your part before you become good at it. Even though there are only a few steps, it can be challenging at first. Your mind may protest this new mental exercise, but soon it will operate so much more effectively and efficiently. If you practice PC regularly, it will become natural and effortless. (I'll give you more ways to use it in the following chapters.) I like to practice PC when I'm grooming a horse, cleaning a stall, or doing some type of activity that is repetitive and requires little conscious thought.

In addition to helping you build your focus muscles, PC can be used to build and test things in your mind before you actually do them. This type of *mind engineering* is a valuable skill to acquire. You can experiment using PC for just about every major decision and task you attempt. This process only takes a few seconds or minutes, but may end up saving you time or effort in the long run.

PC has its own built-in motivation system—as you see results, you'll want to do it more often. Your horse will also enjoy the benefits. Practicing PC will help you rein in your endless supply of thoughts and replace them with the one thought steam you want . . . the productive one.

How to do Productive Contemplation (PC)

Decide on a task you want to complete or a problem you want to solve.

Remove all major distractions (e.g., cell phones and conversation with others).

Breathe deeply and close your eyes for a moment to slow your brain waves.

Imagine going through the motions of completing your task—like you are the writer and director of a movie.

Notice any time you have a thought that is unrelated to the what you want to do—acknowledge the thought and bring your mind back to the task.

Practice staying "on topic" for longer stretches of time.

Notes:

When you first start doing PC, you might begin to notice how often you become distracted by unrelated thoughts and how quickly your mind wanders off.

*With practice, your focus becomes better. You're training your mind to do what **you** want, not what **it** wants!*

You may begin to "see" ways to do the task more efficiently.

Human Thoughts and Horses

Your thoughts affect your horse. Each thought stream you hold creates an emotion in your heart and/or another part of your body.[3] If your thoughts are negative, your horse will have to endure a continual bombardment of negative energy waves from your heart and mind. It can make him anxious or fearful. If you can learn to create positive thoughts and emotions while you ride, your horse will enjoy a steady wave of positive energy from your heart and mind. He will become calm and focused, just like you!

Human energy waves can affect horses even more strongly than they affect other people. As you know, horses are far more sensitive than we are.

When horses interact with humans, they have to do one of two things with the human energy:

1. Ignore it.

2. React to it.
   a) React negatively
   b) React positively

Let's inspect how each of these options influence the horse/human relationship.

Option 1: Horses Who Ignore Human Energy:

Kind and gentle horses who are ridden by a lot of different people, or horses ridden by a rider with a scattered mind but a good heart, often choose Option #1. They essentially ignore the rider. The horse "tunes out" and just goes about doing the job at hand.

Sometimes a horse who is over-trained will also choose Option #1. An over-trained horse is one whose every step is controlled by the rider. Or it's a horse that asked to do something repetitively without a break. They have no down time, so they just tune out and become robotic. Some riders are proud of their robotic, yet obedient horse. But horses who choose this option don't offer their rider any opportunity to connect on a deeper level.

For some horses, Option #1 is not altogether bad. Horses used in therapeutic riding programs perform an important job. They're gentle horses that can handle multiple riders with various physical and mental disabilities. I watched a therapy horse work with four different riders in about an hour. He could let the energy flow through his body and dissipate out his mouth. He yawned frequently, a sign that he was processing and releasing energy. He seemed content and engaged in his work, and not overly stressed.

If you operate an equine-assisted therapy program, keep a close eye on each horse's physical behaviors and state of mind. Horses need a break and down time to recuperate from the constant onslaught of human energy. Giving them regular breaks will help. Ulcers and other health issues or behavioral changes are a good sign they need a break—or a different job.

Option 2a: Horses Who React Negatively to Human Energy:

A horse whose training was rushed or harsh, a horse who endures physical abuse, or a horse who is constantly subjected to negative brain and heart waves from the rider usually chooses Option #2.

It's difficult to predict the ultimate outcome of this scenario, but it's usually not good for the horse or the rider, or both. Maybe you can think of some examples of the negative behaviors that horses exhibit when they have had enough of humans. Horses who choose this option don't form a good relationship with their handler, or a strong connection to humans.

Some show horses also choose this option. A show horse is expected to tolerate not only the heart and brain waves from the rider but also those of all the other anxious horses and riders at a show.

The owner/rider may have high expectations because of how well the horse performs in training. But the weight of the expectations, coupled with the energy of the show, may prove too much for the horse to handle. His only option is to dissipate the excess negative energy.

The horse could do this by shying, spooking, or performing some impressive aerial stunts. He's just trying to get rid of the excess energy, or asking a human to listen. If he internalizes his stress, he may develop ulcers. Dr. Pamela Wilkins of the University of Illinois Veterinary Teaching Hospital has found that more than 90% of performance horses have gastric ulcers![4]

DEBBIE AND BLUE

Debbie brought her roping horse Blue to one of my one-day clinics. Debbie had a lot of stories about Blue. He had been sold several times because he could never quite excel at his owner's chosen sport. Blue was a beautiful athletic horse, but had that checked-out look in his eyes. The look that said he was done with humans and intent on enduring the time he had to spend trying to please his current owner. He wrung his tail throughout the ride. Sometimes he decided to spook, run off, or buck, much to the dismay of Debbie. She told me she didn't trust him and he often scared her, even though she was a competent and confident rider.

In her session, we worked on connection. But Blue was not immediately willing to let go and put his trust in a human. Debbie admitted that he was trained in the rapid method and many fundamentals were skipped along the way. Together, we made a decision to start all over with Blue. We proceeded to treat him like it was his first time under saddle. Debbie rode him at the walk, imagining that she was riding a youngster. She focused on a positive emotion to breathe through her heart. She made pictures in her mind of Blue's feet taking big slow strides while he stayed calm and relaxed in his body. As she relaxed, Blue started to walk with less tension. His head came down. His eyes softened—just a little bit.

Once the walk was nice and relaxed, Debbie made a transition to the trot. Before she asked for the trot, I told her to imagine the feel and speed of the trot she wanted. At first, Blue's trot was fast and Debbie was bouncing quite a bit in the saddle. As she continued to imagine the slow easy jog she desired, Blue started to do it. We focused on keeping him relaxed. No expectations. We were giving him a new way of being with a human.

Debbie understood it was going to take some time to break down the walls of tension Blue had built up. She was more than willing. He was lucky to finally find Debbie, a human who listened.

Option 2b: Horses Who React Positively to Human Energy:

This horse has a rider who has control over his or her thoughts and emotions. Positive heart and brain waves from the human flood over the horse and make him feel good. A true connection and conversation are possible when the horse chooses this option.

If you ever watch Frédéric Pignon and his wife Magali Delgado with their horses, you understand what I'm talking about. They developed Cavalia, a Cirque du Soleil-type show with horses and acrobats.[5] The horses work at liberty and perform spectacularly, despite the intense energy from the audience and the rigors of the show schedule. The communion that these two people have with their horses is extraordinary.

CHERYL AND MONTE

Not all the horses and riders that come to my clinics have problems. Cheryl and Monte made a great team. Cheryl knew that it could be even better . . . or at least easier. It's so much fun to give someone an easy button.

Monte was one of the biggest mustangs I had ever seen. His confidence and power were evident, a testament to Cheryl's good training. She had maintained his personality and mojo.

As Cheryl rode Monte, I looked for places where the energy was stuck. After Cheryl made some small adjustments, Monte's walk, trot, and canter became more relaxed. Then, Cheryl decided to do a leg yield (side pass). To me, it seemed just a bit more work for Cheryl than it needed to be. I had her imagine how she wanted it to feel and how she wanted his feet to move. She kept a clear picture of the leg yield she wanted, and then used her reins, weight, and legs when Monte didn't listen (see). After just a few attempts, they did two perfect leg yields. Smooth, effortless, relaxed, and energetic, with almost no leg or rein cues. Cheryl had a huge smile on her face. She had found the easy button!

Emotions

Emotions are important because they're connected to thoughts. Emotions can either cause a thought or be caused by a thought. The third player in this relationship is a behavior or action. Once an emotion appears, we have to do something in response to it so that it will either stay or go away.[6]

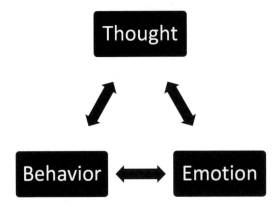

"Positive" emotions are the ones that make us feel wonderful. We like to experience them. Because they make us feel good, we try to recreate them as often as possible. "Negative" emotions make us feel bad, and so we try to run away from them or shut them down.

We tend to put our emotions into categories, labeling them as positive or negative, good or bad. Think of emotions as a nonverbal message from your body. If you shut them off or stuff them down, you lose important information.

If you begin to look at negative emotions as a message from your body that something isn't right, you won't be so quick to cast them off. You'll be able to take steps to correct the problem, and the painful emotion may go away on its own. If you ignore the message for too long, it can show up as physical illness.

If you're plagued by emotions that make you feel bad all the time, it's a good idea to seek help from a professional. Fixing a chronic problem like this is beyond the scope of this book, or my expertise. My focus is on helping you get a handle on those pesky emotions such as fear, doubt, guilt, and anxiety that rear up occasionally when you're interacting with your horse.

The following is a simple technique if you want to get rid of a negative emotion. You'll become better at it the more you practice.

Removing Negative Emotions

The first thing you need to do when you feel a strong negative emotion is recognize the emotion (e.g., sadness, frustration, fear, etc.).

Next, take a few deep breaths, quiet your mind, and ask your body where you feel the pain of that emotion. (It usually settles in an organ or a particular area of your body.)

Continue to breathe deeply and ask the painful emotion what message it has for you. If you can't get anything, ask for assistance from someone you trust. They may be able to help you talk it out.

When you get the message, you can evaluate its meaning.

Once you have received the message and decided what to do, imagine breathing the emotion down through your body and out your feet into the ground. Continue to do this until the feeling lifts.

Example:

You have determined that your emotion is fear. You then quiet your mind and breathe deeply and discover that the throbbing pain is radiating from your solar plexus (stomach). The solar plexus is your power center.

After sitting with the feeling for a few minutes, you find that what you thought was a fear of riding in an arena with a lot of other riders is actually a fear that you'll look less competent than the others. Appearing incompetent in front of your peers would definitely be a blow to your ego and reputation.

If you practice Productive Contemplation, you'll become more aware of your thoughts and emotions. In the next chapter, you'll learn how to include mental imagery in your Productive Contemplation sessions. Once you combine these two powerful practices together, you'll have greater awareness and control over your thoughts, emotions, and behaviors. You'll be able to decide what thoughts and emotions you want to bring with you into your interactions with horses.

The following stories about trailer loading illustrate how profoundly our human thoughts and emotions can affect horses. You can look at the trailer loading as a metaphor for anything you have trouble getting your horse to do.

THE EMOTIONAL SEND-OFF

Vicky hired a trainer to teach her young colts to trailer load. He came to her house several times over a period of a month. At the end of the month, the horses loaded perfectly.

Then, it was time for the colts to leave for their new home. Vicky was overcome with sadness. She cried. She had raised the colts. For her, it was like sending a child off to college. They wouldn't be coming home again. (Well, maybe not exactly like a human child!)

The horse moving van arrived. It took the driver two hours per horse to load the two colts.

THE UNLOADABLE HORSE

After my divorce and an exhausting move to a new home, I was relieved to know that the only things left were my horse trailer and a few small household items. The evening before I planned to leave, my neighbor called.

"Hi, Susie, it's Dawn. Do you have room in your trailer for a horse?"

"Why?" I asked.

"I sold one of my horses to someone near your new house. It would be great if he could catch a ride with you." Dawn paused before adding, "Oh, and by the way, he doesn't load in trailers."

I didn't know how to respond, and finally replied, "I'm leaving at 6:00 in the morning. If he doesn't load, he won't be going with me."

I told Dawn to walk her horse to my place and put him in a stall for the night. In the morning, if he didn't load, she could come pick him up. I suspected the issue wasn't the horse, it was the human. Loading horses into trailers wasn't her forte—she believed that it was hard to get horses into trailers.

That evening, I imagined the horse loading in the trailer. Quick and easy. That morning, I put the horse's halter on and walked him right into the trailer. No fuss. I pulled out of my driveway at 6:00 a.m.

LIA AND BEAU

Lia brought Beau to one of my clinics. Beau was an impressive off-the-track thoroughbred who hid his quiet and willing disposition behind an imposing 17-hand frame. On the first morning of the clinic, I talked about how to establish a heart and mind connection with horses and how to use mental imagery to communicate. In the afternoon, I worked individually with each participant and their horse. In my session with Lia and Beau, we ended up focusing primarily on some physical issues that Beau was experiencing. Throughout the session, he was calm and relaxed. I wasn't yet aware of his problem with horse trailers.

The next morning, I was visiting with the other clinic participants prior to the morning session. From the big picture window in the house, I spotted Lia unloading Beau from her trailer. My friend Rebecca was talking to her as she got Beau settled into a pen. They made their way to the house. I thought nothing of it.

As we all sat down at the big table for the morning discussion, my friend Rebecca seemed a bit unsettled. As I was about to speak, Rebecca politely asked if we could start the morning with a story. She felt that Lia should share with the group what had happened with Beau the previous day. I was taken off guard, a bit nervous about what we were about to hear. At that moment, I didn't know we were going to need a big box of tissue.

Lia was visibly emotional. This seemed strange to me because she was such a strong, confident, and down-to-earth woman. She began by telling us about her past experience with Beau. Beau had always been difficult to load and unload from the trailer — perhaps it reminded him of a bad experience in the starting gate. Whatever the reason for his anxiety, Lia said she always needed help getting him in and out of the trailer. On the way home from clinic the day before, she tried calling several people to help her unload Beau, but nobody was available. She said she started to panic, and then decided to try sending Beau pictures of how she wanted him to unload. When she got to her house, she opened the trailer door, removed the butt bar, and Beau backed out quietly without incident. The next morning, she made pictures of how she wanted him to load, and it was quick and easy. At this point she was crying and so was everyone else. We had to pass around the tissues!

> **Horses believe our thoughts and emotions. Henry Ford said, "Whether you think you can or you can't, either way you are right."[7] Horses change this saying to: "Whether humans think I can or can't, either way I will prove them right."**

CHAPTER 4

Imagine that . . .

"Imagination is the true magic carpet."

—Norman Vincent Peale

When was the last time you watched young children play? I'm not asking if you recall a moment when you observed a child sitting in front of a TV, engaged in a video game, or captivated by an electronic device. Can you remember seeing a child truly play, without the use of technology—and without adults around to create an artificial structure, rules, and time constraints? Have you ever actually seen children who can entertain themselves with their own imagination? It's a rare thing now, so you might have to think back to when you were a child.

One of the childhood games you probably played was the delightful game of Make-Believe. The rules of Make-Believe were simple—there were no rules. When absorbed in the game of Make-Believe, you were in control of the story and the outcome. You could become anything or anyone. If there were other kids involved, you each picked a character to play. The story line evolved organically . . . there was no script. Because there were no rules to the game of Make-Believe, there were no limitations either. The characters could have fantastic adventures without fear of a bad outcome.

Like most horse-crazy girls, I spent a lot of time playing Make-Believe. My spring horse Popcorn and I had amazing adventures. We rounded up cattle in Texas, performed in a circus act, and won the Kentucky Derby. There was nothing we couldn't do together. He was the perfect all-around horse, a beautiful and spirited leopard Appaloosa. He was my friend and constant companion. Make-Believe with Popcorn was my favorite game. But then I grew up and came to understand that the "game" was just for little kids. Popcorn vanished from my life, destined to live out his retirement in the dark attic.

Popcorn at 57 years old.

Even though it's considered a childhood game, many adults still play Make-Believe. They might fantasize about winning the lottery or daydream they're walking on a beach in a beautiful tropical paradise. It's actually hard to give up what most adults think is a waste of time and a silly childhood game. However, sometimes we all need a break from the reality of our lives. There is nothing wrong with playing Make-Believe unless it becomes a dysfunctional way to escape the world.

In the movie, *The Secret Life of Walter Mitty*[1], the main character, played by Ben Stiller, creates an exciting imaginary life. He goes overboard with his daydreaming—to where it actually begins to negatively affect his real life. But in the end, his ability to create realistic daydreams eventually came in handy—it helped him develop confidence and realize his inner hero.

I'm going to encourage you to play a grown-up version of Make-Believe. Not to escape your current reality like Walter Mitty, but to create some positive changes in your riding and relationship with your horse. You can play it anytime you have a few free moments. And it's a wonderful thing to do during your Productive Contemplation time.

Make-Believe is actually a powerful and healthy game for your adult brain. It will help you develop new neural connections or strengthen the ones you want to keep. It's like weight training for your brain! You can use Make-Believe to improve your riding skills or to help you become a more focused rider. The best part about this game is that you can do it anytime and anywhere. And you can improve your riding without having to actually be in the saddle, or even in the proximity of your horse!

You may have heard of the modern grown-up version of Make-Believe. It's often called visualization or mental imagery. Scientists have studied mental imagery for more than 50 years. In study after study, the conclusions are always the same—it works.[2]

> **You truly can change your life—and your horse's life—simply by incorporating mental imagery into your training regime.**

In this chapter, you'll learn why mental imagery works. But first, I want to tell you a story about how a rider used it to imagine her way to multiple national and world championships on her horse. At a single show. Against all odds. In real life!

SUSIE AND TANK

When Tank was born in the spring of 2001, Susie excitedly watched him arrive in the world. When he finally stood up on his long wobbly legs, she couldn't believe how big he was. All the other Morgan foals at the ranch weighed around 65 pounds when they were born. Tank weighed in at a hefty 100 pounds. With his unusually long legs, he towered above the other foals his age. He was solid and strong. His stature earned him his nickname—Tank.

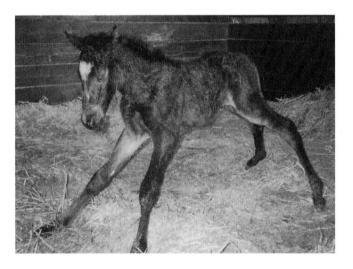

Tank

Tank was actually a gift of sorts. Susie's sister-in-law Kristen had given her his dam when she moved overseas. Kristen owed some money for board, so they agreed that if she gave Susie Tank's dam, it would make everything even. Susie could not have imagined at the time what an awesome gift Kristen had given her.

Susie was a small woman. By the time he turned three, Tank was a whopping 16 hands—huge for a Morgan. Although she started her own horses, Susie's friends questioned whether it was wise for her to start Tank by herself. They recommended she send him out to a cowboy for his initial rides under saddle. In her gut, Susie felt this was a bad idea, and simply wouldn't work. Tank was sensitive, good-minded, and goofy. She was set on keeping him that way, even if it took some time. She recalled, with chagrin, the few horses she had sent to other trainers. They came back trained, but missing an important part of their personality. She was determined not to let this happen to Tank.

Susie wasn't worried about starting Tank. From the time he was a foal, she had worked and played with him. He was always gentle and quick to learn. Tank knew how to ground drive, stand for the farrier, clip, bathe, and load in a trailer. Nothing seemed to rattle him.

Just as she suspected, Tank was easy to start under saddle. She took his training slow, just some walk and trot exercises and easy trail rides his first year. He remained happy and enthusiastic with his work. As a four-year-old, she took him to a local show and competed in a cross-rail class. He loved it and won the class. She took him to some dressage shows and entered him in the walk trot and training level classes. He consistently won those too.

But there was a big problem. It wasn't Tank's problem; it was Susie's. She got so nervous at shows that she would radiate stress and cause him to become anxious. He would whinny, like he was calling attention to her inner turmoil. It was as if he was saying, "Hey, everyone. May I have your attention, please? We have a nervous rider here. Everyone, pay attention!"

Tank's whinnies would make Susie even more anxious. As her anxiety rose, she would freeze during the ride and forget the test pattern. If she had a reader for the test, she would turn the wrong direction. Tank's natural talent caught people's attention, but many of them encouraged Susie to sell him, pointing out that he was too talented a horse for her. She took those outside opinions to heart, and began to believe that she was holding Tank back from reaching his full potential. Everyone's "helpful" suggestions were making the problem worse. Susie knew she either needed to give in and send Tank to a trainer, or she needed to find a way to overcome her show nerves.

Susie was at a crossroads and had some decisions to make. She could: 1) Give up showing; 2) Sell Tank; or 3) Figure out how to fix herself. She decided on #3.

She read and searched the Internet for answers. Then, she remembered something she had done when she was 15 years old. She had listened to a tape on self-hypnosis and it helped her get over her fear of playing her clarinet in front of an audience. It had helped with her school work. And it might help with this problem too.

Susie set aside 30 minutes to an hour every morning to practice Productive Contemplation. Each morning, she played an adult version of Make-Believe. Susie imagined that she and Tank had flawless performances, they easily won their classes, and they both stayed relaxed and fluid during their ride. She made the imagery as real as possible. It was rich in sounds, sights, smells, feelings, and emotions.

It was working! Each show **she** performed better. She had found the answer. But just when things seemed to be coming together, they fell apart. Right before the final show of the season, Susie's world came crashing down. Her husband of 20 years announced that he wanted a divorce. Not only that, he declared that he would leave in a month for his new job. She would be in charge of selling the ranch, the equipment, and all the horses.

Susie found out that their credit cards were cancelled and the bank accounts locked. There was no money. She and Tank had qualified for the Morgan National and World Championship Horse Show in Oklahoma City, but now the possibility of going was fading.

Susie began the process of liquidating the ranch and handling the divorce. She took Tank on a short trail ride each morning, but it was barely enough to keep him in condition. She couldn't focus on training or preparing for the show. She was overwhelmed. It was too hard for her to focus on preparing for a horse show when her life was crumbling down around her.

Then one day she applied for a credit card. To her surprise, she was awarded one in her own name. It arrived in the mail just in time. She loaded up Tank and drove 1,000 miles to Oklahoma City. Susie decided she and Tank would have one last show together.

On the long drive through Kansas, Susie daydreamed. She imagined Tank with long ribbons attached to his bridle and a garland of roses around his neck. In her mind, she saw them making a victory lap in the award ceremony. She felt the exciting buzz of excitement as she imagined accepting the award. She smelled the damp dust in the arena, heard the crowd clapping, and felt the silky ribbon in her hand. Susie let this fantasy steam though her thoughts as she ticked off the miles of corn and wheat fields between her home and the show.

Susie was in a new state of mind, and found she could only recall a few details about the show that week. She remembered that each time she went into the dressage ring she felt intense love and appreciation for Tank. She recalled how much she focused on making their last rides together joyous and stress free. She thought about the deep and enduring gratitude she felt toward Kristen for the gift of Tank's dam. She never even looked at their scores—it didn't matter.

Susie can still remember the feeling of trotting into the big arena for the award ceremony. As Tank took his victory lap, she could hear the long ribbons attached to his bridle flapping in the wind. That weekend, Tank and Susie won several national and world championships. But on the drive home, Susie didn't think about the titles they won—she thought about the warm feeling in her heart. It came from the heart and mind communion she had experienced with Tank.

Susie and Tank

Susie still has Tank. That was their last show, but certainly not their last ride. They now enjoy leisurely trail rides through the mountains, basking in a communion most equestrians long for. One day, Susie will weep as she lays Tank to rest. But she will never have to part with the memories of their adventures together. After all, she can always meet with him again—in a daydream.

The Science of Make-Believe
(aka—Mental Imagery)

You may wonder how imagining something can bring it into existence. It's really not as magical as it might seem. When scientists developed sophisticated brain imaging technology, they could finally observe what happens in peoples' brains when they imagine. What neuroscientists found was mind-blowing. They discovered that the brain doesn't know the difference between reality and Make-Believe![3]

For decades now, neuroscientists have compared the brains of people while they are engaged in an activity verses when they just imagine they're doing that same activity. There is no noticeable difference—the same areas of the brain become activated.[4]

Scientists love experiments, so they have tested this phenomenon out in different ways. Neuroscientist and psychiatrist, Dr. Norman Doidge found that:

> . . . when people close their eyes and visualize a simple object, such as the letter a, the primary visual cortex lights up in the brain scan, just as it would if the people were actually looking at the letter a, and this happens with complex imagery as well. (p.214–215)[5]

The visual cortex is not the only area of the brain that becomes activated during mental imagery. In 2003, researchers at the Karolinska Institute in Stockholm, Sweden, found that this activation also applies to muscle movement. These researchers had test subjects move different parts of their body. They observed on the imaging technology what areas of the brain became activated. Then, they had these same people just imagine they were moving those same body parts without actually moving their body at all. The brain scans looked almost identical![6]

Taking this concept a little further, researchers Shackell and Standing conducted an experiment to see if people could improve their muscle strength through mental imagery. They picked muscles in the hip that are difficult to strengthen without doing a specific exercise (i.e., the iliacus and psoas muscles). They had one group of participants doing hip flexor exercises for 15 minutes a day, 5 days a week, for 2 weeks. Another group did the same thing, but merely imagined they were doing the exercise. A third group of participants were the control group. They did nothing for the 2 weeks.

Shackle and Standing tested all the participants before and after the experiment. Not surprisingly, the control group had no change in muscle strength. The group of people who did the hip flexor exercise increased their muscle strength by 28.3%. Amazingly, the group who only imagined they were doing the exercise increased their muscle strength by 23.7%![7] (This is not an excuse to become a couch potato!)

What happens when you combine mental imagery with physical training?

The results are even more astonishing. In 2005, researchers Brouziyne and Molinaro tested this on a group of beginner golfers. They wanted to see if mental imagery combined with physical practice could help the golfers improve a new skill—the chip shot.

Brouziyne and Molinaro divided the golfers into three groups. The first group practiced their chip shot and imagined practicing their chip shot. The second group only practiced their chip shot on the golf course. The group third did nothing. The golfers who combined physical practice with mental imagery had the most improvement, followed by the group who just practiced their chip shot on the golf course.[8]

These are just a few examples of the thousands of studies done on the effectiveness of mental imagery. Scientists agree that the greatest benefit comes by combining mental imagery with physical practice.[9]

How can you use mental imagery to help you and your horse?

The answer is: The possibilities are almost limitless. Let me give you some examples. Let's say you just learned a new riding skill or technique. When you learned it, your brain created a new neural connection for that skill. You want to make that neural connection stronger, so you repeat that skill as often as you can. The problem is, if you do it on your horse, he or she could become tired or annoyed—or your mount does the movement incorrectly.

Here's the solution. When you learn the new skill and you can do it well at least one time, stop and sit on your horse. (Make sure you did it right. You don't want to strengthen a neural connection for doing it wrong!) Imagine doing the skill perfectly again and again in your mind. Feel what it is like in your body when you do it correctly. As you imagine, include as many details as possible and as many of your senses as you can. Practice—in your mind—whenever you have a few free moments.

You strengthen the neural connection each time you imagine. Soon, the neural connection will be so strong that you don't have to think anymore and the skill will become automatic. Congratulations—you've constructed a neural super-highway to your new destination (skill)! Unfortunately, if you have a bad habit you want to break, you have to make the neural connection extra strong so that it overrides the one for doing it wrong.[10] Your brain is like a computer—it always wants to default to the original programming.

Another way you can strengthen the neural connection for the skill you want is by watching someone who is an expert and does the task correctly. When you watch another person, your brain will fire the same neurons as if you were doing it.[11] This is because the brain has mirror neurons. These neurons help young children learn by watching others. Babies use mirror neurons to mimic the facial expressions of an adult.[12] Mirror neurons still exist in your adult brain, so put them to use!

You can also use mental imagery as you ride. Make a habit of using mental "pre-cues"—pictures in your mind of what you want your horse to do. (I'll explain mental and energetic pre-cues in greater detail in the next chapter.) Create feelings in your body of how you want it to feel. See or imagine your horse doing it just as you want. Keep your emotions positive and reward him when he does what you imagined. Make sure you don't imagine doing it wrong, or imagine what could go wrong. While doing this, it's important to keep out all other thoughts and emotions that distract you or negatively impact the image. This means you have to be aware of any negative self-talk (i.e., that pesky voice in your head that tries to make you doubt yourself).

Be patient with yourself as you practice mental imagery when riding or interacting with your horse. Just like any skill, it takes practice before you can perfect it. Once your body and mind are in alignment with what you want your horse to do, he'll start paying attention to your imagery. When you begin to incorporate pre-cues before applying a physical cue, you may find that your horse is quicker to respond to your request and it becomes easier to teach him new things. Even if you don't believe that horses can "see" the pictures in your head, they can detect the physiological changes in your body when you imagine. Imagining does one other important thing—it keeps **your** mind focused on what you are doing. You unintentionally practice *intention*. (More about intentions in Chapter 5.)

When you imagine, there will be a thought and emotion attached to it.[13] Thoughts and emotions create a physiological response in your body.[14] They influence your breathing, heart rate, and galvanic skin response (GSR). (GSR is a measure of how well your skin conducts electricity.[15] A lie detector machine measures changes in GSR.)

As the images in your head change and create different thoughts and emotions, the tension in your muscles change. The electromagnetic energy waves emitted by your heart and brain change. And your GSR changes.[16] Your horse notices and feels all of these small changes, even if you don't. He or she is one big hairy lie detector machine, heart rate monitor, and biofeedback/neurofeedback machine!

If you want to rid yourself of show nerves, fear, or some other unwanted behavior or emotion, put your imagination to work. Spend time in your Productive Contemplation to imagine that you and your horse perform perfectly. You could envision that he goes by the arena gate without trying to bolt out, or any other thing you want to experience. Just like a child playing Make-Believe, create a story for the way you want your riding and relationship with your horse to be like. Exercise your mental imagery skills as often as possible. Even if you only have a few seconds or minutes, you can do a flash imagery. Keep in mind — the more you practice, the better you'll get at making effective and detailed mental pictures. Remember, your brain doesn't know the difference between reality and what you imagine. Strengthen those neural connections for what you want, not what you don't want!

Elite athletes use mental imagery as a secret weapon. (Begin to notice how often great athletes talk about their "mental game.") They know that it gives them the advantage over their opponents, especially when times get tough. But mental imagery is not just for athletes. It helps cultivate qualities such as confidence, concentration, focus, and patience.[17]

**Benefits of making mental imagery
a regular practice:**[18]

Enhanced focus and concentration

Heightened creativity

Greater problem-solving skills

Energy boost

Elevated level of self-confidence

Consistent positive moods

Better health

Faster healing

Improved performance (sport, fitness, academic, work)

Faster recovery from injury or illness

Reduced stress and anxiety

How to Make-Believe Like a Child!

Just in case you have forgotten how to play Make-Believe, here are some important guidelines (Remember, there are no rules to this game!):

• Think about what you would like to improve, how you would like your horse to behave, or how you would like a situation to turn out.

• Create a story about it. The story can be as short as a few minutes, or as long as you like. Include a beginning, middle, and an end for your story.

Make Believe: *The ability to create a realistic, controllable, and interactive model of an event or desired outcome in your imagination. This mental model feels real because it is created using all five senses, along with a strong positive emotion. It is fueled by an unwavering belief that the event or outcome will happen just as imagined . . . or even better!*
—Susan D. Fay, PhD

Creating a Story

1. Make a list of the things you see.

Create as much detail as you can. For example, what are your surroundings like? What do you and your horse look like? What do you see yourselves doing? Is it day or night, cloudy or clear?

You can imagine that you are seeing it out of your own eyes, or you can pretend you are looking at yourself from above or out of another person's eyes. Choose the perspective that works best for you. You can even switch back and forth between them depending on the situation.

2. Make a list of things you hear.

Include the surrounding noises.

Imagine what you want to hear people say.

Hear what you would say to yourself out loud or in your head.

3. Make a list of things you feel in your body.

For example, how do you move your hands, legs, feet, and body? What does the horse feel like to you as he moves? What does it feel like when you touch him?

What is the temperature of the air, the feel of your clothes, etc.?

3. Make a list of the smells that surround you.

Maybe you smell fresh shavings in a stall.

Notice the smell of trees or the aroma of the arena footing.

Conjure up the familiar smell of your horse.

4. Include anything you might taste.

Perhaps it's a cup of coffee before your ride, or your favorite snack after your ride.

Notice the taste of the clean air.

5. Now, decide how you want to feel inside.

What strong positive emotion will you feel at the end of your story?

Let the excitement of success permeate your body.

Notes:

You want to make your imagery as realistic as possible.

It helps if you slow down your imagery when you're trying to perfect a new skill. That way, you can concentrate on all the steps or small movements required.

Once you have a skill down, just run your imagery in real time.

Imagine yourself riding or working your horse in various conditions (e.g., wind, rain, other horses/activity).

Mental imagery works best if done often and consistently.

If you don't "see" images, don't despair. Simply close your eyes and imagine, or just think about your story. Your imagery may just be a series of thoughts at first. Pretend that you CAN see the images. Even if you don't think it's working, stay at it.

Example of a Story

The following Make-Believe story is the one that Susie daydreamed about on her way to the big show in Oklahoma City. The ellipsis (. . .) in this story mean that there was a pause so that the image or feelings could be created and experienced.

I can feel the excitement in my body, the butterflies and tingles extend from my head to my toes . . . Tank and I are in line behind a bay horse, ready to go into the big bright arena . . . We are about to make a victory lap . . . Against all odds, Tank won all of his classes! . . . I can see the beautiful long ribbons attached to each side of Tank's bridle . . . They have blue rosettes with three long white ribbons streaming down . . . I can see the writing on each . . . Champion . . . Around Tank's neck are two garlands of red roses . . . I can feel him breathing deeply

*and hear him softly snorting as we wait to enter the arena . . .
I hear the announcer on the loud speaker call our names . . . I
say to myself, "I'm so excited about what we have accomplished
together.". . . As he trots into the arena, I can feel the power of
his stride under my seat. It feels as if we are floating on air . . .
The wood mulch beneath his hooves is soft . . . As his hooves
land in the cushy footing, they make no sound . . . The smell of
the damp wood mulch creates a musty smell that fills my nostrils . . . I taste the damp, woody air on my tongue as I breathe
. . . As we trot to the end of the arena, I can hear applause from
the crowd . . . The air in the arena feels muggy, but the ribbons
on Tank's bridle create a gentle breeze that cools my face . . .
As we stop to receive our awards, I see the flash of the photographer's camera as he takes our picture . . . My heart is burst-
ing with joy, gratitude, and love . . . I'm so grateful to have
Tank!*

Susie and Tank — Victory Lap

This story included all the senses—plus a positive and powerful emotion. Susie commented afterward that the real experience was eerily similar to her daydream.

The Make-Believe stories that you create for your Productive Contemplations may not be as elaborate as this one. They may be as simple as imagining you can easily catch your horse, that you can ride past a scary object as if it wasn't there, or you can perfect a new maneuver. Just have fun with Make-Believe. You're only limited by your own imagination! The topic and the outcome are up to you. As you see positive results, you may soon find yourself daydreaming . . . much more often.

CHAPTER 5

Clear the Air(waves): Intentions and Pre-Cues

"An intention is not a goal. A goal is something you want to accomplish in the future. An intention is a desire for how you want things to be—in the present moment."

—Susan D. Fay, PhD

I called up my friend Ally, anxious to hear about the progress she was making with her new 3-year-old gelding. After a few minutes of small talk, she told me her goal was to have a first ride on Sly soon. There was a long hesitation, as if she was trying to find just the right words. Finally, she blurted out, "I'm so frustrated with Sly. It's almost impossible to lead him because he's constantly pulling me from one clump of green grass to the next. When I try to correct him, he gets all emotional and out of control. I can't help but let my emotions follow his, and our time together always escalates into a big fight. I just don't need another struggle in my life. I have to argue with people all day at work and I'm so tired of conflict . . ." She finally took a breath and her voice trailed off. I could hear her sniffles.

I didn't answer immediately, wondering if it was appropriate to offer some assistance. I felt the familiar internal nod (from my gut), so when it seemed like the time was right, I inquired if she wanted some help with Sly. With what sounded like a huge sigh of relief, Ally replied, "I thought you would never ask!"

Before hanging up the phone, I agreed to meet Ally at the stable where she boarded Sly. I decided it would be best if the two of them didn't begin the day with a potential argument over getting into the horse trailer. We could focus on trailer loading after we dealt with the leading issue, but I guessed they were related. Once you address the root cause of one problem in the relationship—whether it comes from the human or the horse—many unwanted horse behaviors miraculously disappear.

On the 2-hour drive to the stable, my mind went over several scenarios for dealing with Sly's emotional and behavioral problems. Even though I had trained horses for more than 30 years, each situation, each horse, and each owner offered me a new opportunity to explore the reason behind a breakdown in the horse-human connection. Relationships are like a jigsaw puzzle—it's often difficult or time consuming to assemble all the pieces to create a beautiful picture. It was my intention to help Ally put some pieces back together and resurrect her relationship with Sly.

I had just pulled into the parking space at the stable when I spotted Ally eagerly waving to me and gesturing the way to Sly's stall. It was a sunny day, so when I entered the barn it took a few seconds for my eyes to adapt to the darkness. There were no windows in the barn to filter in light from the outside, so I could only make out the silhouette of Ally at the far end of a long row of stalls. I saw her grab a halter and horse cookie before sliding open a heavy wooden door. A horse with a chiseled jaw and delicate muzzle popped his head out. I saw him greedily push his nose into Ally's hand and grab the treat before quickly retreating to the back corner of his stall. By the time I got to the end of the barn aisle and peered inside at Sly, all I could see was a muscular Quarter Horse rear end and a long magnificent tail. It wasn't the welcome I had hoped for!

Ally started to walk into the stall to catch Sly when I stopped her. Startled, she halted mid stride. I suggested we let him catch us. She turned to look at me with a perplexed expression on her face, muttering softly, "Like that's ever going to happen!"

Ally and I stood by the open stall door. Sly continued to stand in the back corner without moving a muscle, as if he hoped we couldn't see him and would decide to leave. In truth, I ignored him and asked Ally to do the same. I directed Ally to focus on her breathing, slowing it down as we talked. Once she was breathing deeply, slowly, and regularly, we both focused on a positive emotion and imagined it coming from our hearts. After a few moments, Ally was able to let go of the mind chatter in her head. (Remember thoughts follow emotions.) As soon as she felt relaxed, we placed our focus on Sly. In our minds, we set a silent intention that he would come to us. He did. Ally was astonished. We had cleared the airwaves, connected to Sly, and opened up the lines of communication. Now we had to practice leading him—with *intention*.

Ally put the halter on Sly and tried to lead him out of the stall. He forced his way past her, rushing to the spot where she kept a bucket of horse treats. He ignored her verbal requests to stop as she jerked his head away from the cookies with the lead rope. Exasperated, she exclaimed, "See what I mean? This is how the fight starts. It continues to get worse for both of us until I put him away."

I told her take Sly back into the stall and focus on her breathing and emotions, the same exercise we did to get him to come to us. I took the lead rope, established an intention that Sly would walk politely out of his stall and stand quietly next to me. The first step we took toward the door, he tried to bolt and I corrected him—without a change in my emotions—and continued to maintain my intention. He seemed startled for a moment and then did just what I asked. By watching him enter and exit the stall nicely several times, Ally could see that he was capable of doing it without drama. She took the lead rope back and practiced the same thing, this time with clear intention. He became a different horse. A smile began to appear on Ally's face.

We practiced making a clear intention that Sly would keep his attention on Ally and respectfully lead past green grass, a bucket of horse cookies, and other horses. Because he could quickly get away from Ally, I had her stop him whenever she felt his energy start to escalate. She learned to breathe deeply and slowly and wait until she felt his energy level come down before going forward. In the process, she became more aware of his emotional state—and hers. And she discovered a way to stop his unwanted emotionally-driven behaviors before they became too difficult for her to control. In the process, she built in a relaxation button—for both of them. She learned how to remain steady in her emotions and not let Sly rattle her. His emotional outbursts had become a way for him to get out of doing something. He had figured out his behavior would scare Ally and she would put him away.

After a short time, Sly was completely connected to Ally and she was leading him calmly and with purpose. He was no longer trying to run over her, snatch a bite of grass, or bolt off. His eyes became softer and Alley became more confident because she had a new powerful tool at her disposal—*intention*.

Sly relaxed more and more the longer we interacted with him. We made a decision to saddle him up and take him to the round pen. Even though he had been saddled many times, we still made pictures and set an intention for what we were going to do before we did it. In the round pen, we put Sly through several ground maneuvers, checking in often to make sure our attention was on him and his attention was on us. We also made sure our thoughts and emotions were in alignment with our intentions.

He stayed soft in his body and didn't whinny for his friends back at the barn. Ally found this remarkable. She told me he usually got more and more anxious and disconnected from her the longer she worked him in the round pen.

In his new calm state, it seemed that Sly was enjoying spending time with us. Ally's 6-year-old granddaughter Emma, who had been watching all the time, asked if she could sit on Sly. At first, I was hesitant, but based on Sly's behavior and demeanor, I thought it would be safe. (I trusted my gut.) I asked Ally and she agreed. She had Emma strap on her helmet and I showed Ally how to quickly remove Emma if necessary. Before Emma got on, we made a mental picture for Sly of Emma sitting in the saddle and we maintained an intention that he would stay relaxed.

When Emma slid into the saddle, Sly had no reaction. I led him around the round pen while Ally walked along side in case we needed to abort the mission. Sly walked with his head low and his eyes half closed. Emma's joy seemed to ooze from every pore of her body. It was contagious. We all walked slowly back to the barn—Sly included—blanketed in a warm bubble of energy. We had all experienced communion in the sacred space.

Disclaimer: Never engage in a session such as this unless you're a highly experienced equestrian with years of experience starting and training horses.

I don't advocate trying this type of thing without expert supervision and a thorough understanding of equine behavior. Throughout the session, I made sure that we took every precaution possible to ensure the safety of all people and horses.

Intention

By holding an intention in your mind—a plan of what you're going to do—it changes the physiology in your body. Your posture changes to reflect your intention. When you align clear thoughts and positive emotions with your intentions, it gives your horse a reliable "leader" to follow. (More about the concept of leadership in Chapter 11.)

Birds in murmuration are an excellent example of intention in action. In murmuration, hundreds—or thousands—of birds (usually starlings) fly together in unison. They create beautiful undulating patterns in the sky that appear as if they have been intricately choreographed and meticulously rehearsed. Watching this phenomenon in action is both awe-inspiring and unbelievable. Many years ago, traveling through De Beque Canyon on my way to Grand Junction, Colorado, I witnessed a starling murmuration. It was so spectacular that people stopped and got out of their cars to watch the aerial ballet performed by of flock of small, ordinary black birds. It was hard to imagine how they pulled off such a feat without crashing into each other. They had to be totally and completely connected—with intention. (You can find numerous videos of starlings in murmuration on the Internet.)

In 2010, a team of theoretical physicists from the University of Rome, led by Dr. Giorgio Parisi, published a research paper on starling murmuration. In their scientific article, they stated, "The change in the behavioral state of one animal affects and is affected by that of all other animals in the group, no matter how large the group is."[1] They further explained that the velocity of one bird affects the velocity of all the others, theorizing that murmuration works much like ferromagnetism, a phenomenon whereby particles in a magnet exhibit perfect interconnection at a critical temperature (or in the case of starling murmuration, some other critical factor).[2]

In a review of Parisi's article, Wired Science reporter Brandon Keim added, "In particle physics, synchronized orientation is found in systems with 'low noise', in which signals are transmitted without degrading."[3] (This may be one explanation for why Ally's horse responded to our brain and heart waves once we stopped our mind chatter and placed our focus on him.)

In another study conducted in 2012, Dr. George Young and his research team studied the influence of orientation—how a change in direction of one bird affects the other birds around it. His team found that an individual bird influences the movement of the seven birds nearest to it . . . and each of those seven, in turn, affect seven birds next them.[4] You can see this effect in action if you watch the starlings in murmuration. There are often several different "clouds" of birds within the larger murmuration, each moving together as a cohesive group. When we have a clear intention and we're truly connected to our horse—heart-to-heart and mind-to-mind—it's possible that we become the leader who influences the movement of the "group."

It's an awesome feeling when you and your horse experience a form of human-equine murmuration and begin dancing together in unison and grace. Although it may look like magic to others, you know there is a scientific explanation for what is happening. Because the connection is scientifically-based, it can be reproduced. But it takes practice, especially if you have previously interacted with your horse unconsciously (without intention).

While riding or interacting with your horse, consciously focus on producing mental pictures, controlling your thoughts and emotions, and maintaining intentions for what you want your horse to do. You'll begin to notice positive changes—in you and your horse. Remember to hold in your mind an unwavering belief that your horse will follow your mental pictures and intentions. When he does what you ask, praise him with your voice, a gentle pat, and an energetic *Thank You* in the form of a burst of positive emotion.

As you practice and experiment, you may begin to wonder why this skill set isn't taught and/or emphasized by more equestrian instructors. Once you get good at it—and remember to do it every time you interact with your horse—you'll feel more powerful. But the power doesn't come from force. It's an invisible strength that is only available to those who can consciously access the energy field.

You can set intentions for almost anything you plan to do. An intention helps you stay focused on a desired outcome. Be careful not to have an intention of control because that is a form of force. The energy behind the need for something to turn out a certain way, or the intention to force a particular demand, can actually create a block in the energy flow. If the energy that drives your intention is to experience a positive emotion, you stay soft on the outside and strong on the inside. Your horse is more likely to willingly follow your request when you operate with an energy of power rather than one of force.

Start playing with intentions to get a feel for how they work for you. For example, I set an intention at my clinics that everyone will be safe and support each other. I choose a positive heart energy emotion that fits the situation or group. I also make sure to set an intention that each participant will receive, see, hear, or experience something that is of value to them. I purposely create a sacred space of positive energy. The surprising thing is that something unexpected and mind-blowing always happens when this is my intention.

The Energy Bubble

Thus far, you've learned about how to use energy to connect with your horse and begin a discussion. Another way to use energy to communicate with your horse when riding, leading, or doing ground work is to make an imaginary oval of moving energy around you and/or your horse. You change the size, speed, and direction of this energy bubble depending on the maneuver you're doing. (See the figures below for an example of what your energy bubble might look like in your mind.)

Energy
Bubble—Extended Gait

Energy Bubble—Collected Gait

When you consciously direct the energy bubble, it works in a similar way to intention. It puts your mind and body into alignment for what you are doing—it removes any "noise" and creates an unobstructed path for the energy to flow. Once you're able to create a consistent and smooth flow of energy around you and your horse, it becomes an incredible invisible aid that works in conjunction with your physical aids.

The use of the energy bubble can become quite sophisticated, but it's important to first understand how to do it and experiment with your horse. Once you become familiar with the concept, you'll probably be able to dream up a myriad of ways to use it. Remember to always make a picture in your mind of what you want your horse to do, put a feel of it in your body, keep your thoughts and emotions under control, hold an intention, and imagine a bubble of energy surrounding you both. Add physical aids last, and only if necessary. Eventually you want your horse to listen to the invisible energy, but this will happen only if you practice and remain consistent in your energy aids.

Examples of how to imagine the energy flow inside the bubble:

To slow your horse down, imagine the energy in the bubble moving at a reduced speed.

To stop, do the same thing but stop the energy flow in the bubble and imagine sending it down into the ground.

To create more forward momentum, run a horizontal bubble of energy and imagine the energy flow moving faster or projecting further out in front of you.

To create a more collected move, imagine the oval of energy flowing up (vertically) rather than forward.

Energetic Pre-Cues

Pre-cues are exactly that—a cue before the main aid is applied. For our purposes, think of the pre-cue as a change in your energy bubble, mind pictures, and intention before you apply a physical aid. An energetic pre-cue could be a brief hesitation or change in the direction of the energy flow in the bubble, along with a quick insertion of a new mind picture or intention.

You can do an energetic pre-cue to correct an unwanted behavior, to ask your horse to become more collected, or to get his attention. You are probably already doing something similar to this, but without conscious intention. Be assured, the horse is fully aware each time your energy changes. If it happens too often, your horse has no choice but to tune out the signals, just as he would if you were unconsciously bouncing your hands on the reins, or mindlessly kicking his sides with your heels. The energy changes and mind pictures would have no meaning, so the horse would learn to ignore them—probably for his own protection and sanity! Now that you know about the energy bubble and intentions, you're going to pay attention and make conscious and intentional energetic pre-cues.

When you begin to make conscious energy changes in yourself, you'll be able to start communicating with your horse on an entirely new level. You can quickly and easily learn to be conscious of the energy you're projecting because your horse will let you know through his behavior. When you become good at controlling and directing your energy, you'll be able influence and inspire the behavior or movement you'd like to create in your horse. Once you're aware of the energy and visualizations you're sharing with your horse, your communication and connection will improve dramatically—sometimes to the point of being unbelievable. But it's a natural response that happens all the time, whether you're aware of it or not. Once you understand the science behind this invisible cue, you can feel confident in your ability to consciously use it as another way to have a meaningful conversation with your horse.

Using Mental Imagery as a Pre-Cue

The ability to see or make pictures in your mind may not come naturally to you. It certainly didn't for me. I was always frustrated when someone would tell me to close my eyes and visualize because all I would see was complete blackness. After I relaxed and allowed myself to just imagine, I realized that my "images" came in the form of a strong knowing. With lots of time and practice, I eventually turned those "knowings" into mind pictures. If you struggle to visualize, just sit for a moment and imagine something. Soon you'll start to notice how your mind "pictures" things. Maybe you feel it in your body, or you somehow "hear" it, or maybe you just know. Any of the forms your imagery takes are valid.

CRUSH AND MENTAL PRE-CUES

By the time my three-year-old black stallion was ready to start, I had become quite good at flexing my imagination muscles and making mental pictures. Before doing anything with him, I made mental pre-cues of what we were about to do. I wasn't sure if he was gentle and willing by nature, or if it was a result of our connection and my ability to have an energetic conversation with him. Back then, I didn't have names for what I was doing, nor did I understand the science behind why it worked. I just did it.

Although I had handled him almost every day of his life, I knew mounting Crush for the first time by myself was still a risky endeavor. It would be foolish to think any horse is safe 100% of the time. I put on my helmet, making sure I was mentally and emotionally relaxed and that my breathing was slow and deep. The first ride is always a big moment in a horse's life. It can set the stage for his future behavior and his attitude toward people and his work. My **intention** was to make Crush's first ride a positive and stress-free experience for him—and me!

I started out by making pictures of putting on Crush's saddle and bridle while he remained calm and relaxed. I imagined him walking up to the mounting block and standing still. (He was already good at this.) Then, I imagined putting my foot in the stirrup and swinging my leg over him before settling into the saddle. Again, I painted an image in my mind of him calmly standing still and then walking off quietly when I gently closed my legs around his sides. I recalled good rides on other horses, helping me maintain my positive thoughts and emotions.

Crush's first ride

My first ride on Crush was just as I imagined—quiet and uneventful. While taking off the saddle, he lowered his head and chewed. It was as if he had been ridden hundreds of times before. Thinking back on that day, I had prepared him for years for his first ride. From the day he was born, I had imagined how wonderful it would be to ride him. Maybe he had picked up all those "pre" pre-cues!

Training with and without Pre-Cues

In contrast to the relaxed and low stress experience that Crush had for his first ride under saddle, other horses are not as lucky. Often trainers take young horses into a round pen where they are saddled and ridden after being run to the point of near exhaustion. It's a good guess that the trainer didn't prepare the horse for the experience by using mental pre-cues. The trainer may expect the horse to buck—and unintentionally make mental pictures of him doing just that. They may expect the horse to be fearful, unaware that they're creating fear by their aggressive energy or the fact that the horse doesn't have any idea of what to expect.

The overwhelm and feelings of fear some trainers create in a horse may cause him to either fight, bolt off, or shut down. None of these responses are necessary or desirable. (Refer back to the section on horse's reaction to human energy in Chapter 3.) When a horse experiences fear, it often creates a block or brace in his mind and body that is difficult to remove later. A rapid and thoughtless start may cause a horse to mentally shut down and become robotic or ignore the rider's cues. If this is the case, he gives the trainer the illusion of being safe and obedient, but it's difficult to predict what might set him off in the future. Other horses who are started this way may become dangerous and/or unpredictable, always ready to flee from the human or prepare for the next fight. A horse subjected to forceful or rapid training isn't broke, he's broken—in heart and spirit.

If you want to start your horse and interact in a gentler and more respectful way, learn how to make clear pictures in your mind and send them to your horse as a pre-cue. The mental pre-cues aren't a substitute for horse handling skills and knowledge, but you'll find it enhances them. Your mental pre-cues will also help you become more focused during your interactions with your horse. It's also a polite way to let your horse know what the two of you are about to do. Once you begin using mental pre-cues on a regular basis—in a conscious way—you'll wonder why you never did it before. You'll discover what a simple and valuable tool it is, especially when training your horse to do anything new—from loading in a trailer to clean flying lead changes.

Creating Mental Pre-Cues

You learned about mental imagery in Chapter 4. If you review the section in that chapter on creating a story, this will help you develop highly effective mind pictures to use as pre-cues. Most importantly, remember to picture what you want your horse to do, not what you don't. The following is a short reminder of the steps to making good mind pictures:

- Make an intention for what you want to accomplish.
- Feel it in your own body.
- See it in your mind.
- Add a positive emotion to the picture.
- See it from your horse's perspective.
- Feel and see it from your perspective.
- Visually run through the entire action. (Once you get good at single pictures, put them together into a running movie while you ride.)
- Imagine your horse doing it perfectly.
- Believe, without a doubt, your horse will do it correctly in a relaxed manner.
- Reward your horse when he does what you want (send a burst of positive energy).
- Pay attention to changes in your horse that would indicate he received and understood your mind picture.

- Check in often on your thoughts and emotions and make sure they're positive.
- Hold an expectation of success—if you have doubts, your horse will pick up on them.
- Trust that visualization works.
- Practice.
- Experiment.
- Be patient. (Becoming good at visualization takes time.)
- Stay relaxed and have fun!

CHAPTER 6

Coming to Your Senses

"Magic is really only utilization of the entire spectrum of the senses."

—Michael Scott, *The Alchemyst*

A cknowledging that humans have more than just five senses is a relatively new paradigm. The hit 1999 movie *The Sixth Sense*[1] left most viewers shocked at the end. For many of us, it wasn't as shocking that the boy could see dead people as it was that we had missed all the subtle clues throughout the movie. The movie title should have been our biggest hint!

You may not know anyone who can see dead people. But perhaps you know someone who possesses some type of super human sense. My mother was one such person. She had an uncanny ability to smell a fire, even if it was miles away. One quiet summer day, she insisted that there was a forest fire near our home in the mountains. The whole family piled into the car, and we drove for about an hour through the dense Colorado pine trees with the windows rolled down. My mom, with her head out the window, would tell my dad which road to take and where to turn. Sure enough, we eventually came upon a small abandoned campfire. We smothered the fire with dirt, possibly preventing a forest fire. During the entire drive, no one else in the car could detect any hint of smoke. My mom was frustrated with the rest of us because to her, the smell of fire was overpowering!

Super human senses can be found in the most ordinary of people. One such person was a park ranger in Florida. On the island where we worked, dogs weren't allowed. Somehow, he instantly knew if someone had smuggled a dog into the park. He would look up from what he was doing and announce, "There's a dog on the island!" He would jump in his truck and drive right to the dog. He served as the park's official "bloodhound." And he was never wrong. His superhuman sense allowed him to detect the presence of a dog more than a mile away!

So how do people develop seemingly super human senses?

One theory is that they trained their brain to pay attention to subtle environmental clues—clues that are too minute for the basic five senses to detect without a boost from the emotional center of the brain.[2] The thought of a forest fire terrified my mom, so she honed her sense of smell. Her subconscious mind was constantly scanning the environment for any hint of smoke. She became highly tuned to detect the slightest smell of smoke. The park ranger hated dogs, so his brain was constantly scanning the environment for anything that might suggest a dog was around.

You can probably think of people, like my mom and the park ranger, who have a heightened sense of smell, touch, taste, feel, or sight. If you want to improve one of your senses, then just start placing your attention on detecting information from that sense. It helps in the beginning to take away one of your other senses. For example, close your eyes or put in ear plugs. This takes away some of the distracting information coming in from the environment. Keep your attention focused on that one thing. Notice everything you sense about that thing. Tell yourself, "I'll smell, taste, feel, hear, see, or somehow notice if _____ (fill in the blank) is around." If you add a strong emotion, that will help. In the examples above, both people had a strong negative emotion that led them to develop a heightened sense. But the emotion doesn't have to be negative to work. If you imagine a strong **positive** emotion, this will also work to heighten your sense(s).

Think about a time that you focused your brain in on a particular topic. Let's say, for example, it's a certain type of saddle that you would love to own. With your brain focused on that saddle and the emotion (i.e., I'd love to have one), you begin to see that saddle everywhere. This happens because you told your brain to focus on it. Then, your subconscious mind started to scan the environment for that saddle. It brought it to your attention (conscious mind) when it detected that particular saddle. It may not be that there are actually more of those saddles—it's just that now you notice them.

If you paid attention to everything in your environment, you would soon become overwhelmed. Every single second, your senses are picking up more than 11 million bits of information.[3] Your conscious mind can't possibly pay attention to 11 million things at once. Therefore, your subconscious mind developed a way to scan the environment for what is important to notice. The information received by your senses that isn't necessary for survival, pertinent to completing the task at hand, or something you directed your brain to notice, never reaches your conscious mind.[4] In essence, these other things are invisible, a phenomenon known as inattentional blindness.[5]

Researchers found that often people don't hear or see something unless they expect it. They can also experience inattentional blindness if they are thinking about an unrelated topic, or their attention is focused elsewhere.[6] Arien Mack, PhD, the researcher who developed the theory of inattentional blindness, discovered that a person must place their attention on something before their conscious mind can perceive it.[7]

People with the super human ability to focus in a loud environment have just programed their subconscious mind in an opposite way—to ignore everything except the thing they are focusing on.[8] Imagine how handy this skill would be in many different areas of your life. You can teach yourself to do it, especially now that you know how your brain works.

When women complain that their husband never pays attention to them when they talk, it could be that their husband has developed a super human ability to tune out his wife's voice. Or his subconscious mind automatically filters out all the things he doesn't consider important. In reality, he can't hear her! He has an inattentional hearing deficit!

You can play with programming your subconscious to start paying attention with specific intent. For example, you might get in the car and tell yourself, *I'm going to notice all the cars with an out-of-state license plate.* This is probably something that doesn't matter to you. It's certainly not important to your survival. But as you drive to your destination, suddenly you can't stop seeing lots of cars from other states!

The "Other" Senses

Are there people who have more than five senses? The answer is undeniably yes. We all do!

Our ancestors could detect many more things than we can—probably because their life depended on their ability to sense danger, changes in the weather, where to find food, etc. They also didn't have technology to distraction them. We have "lost" those senses only because we no longer pay attention to them. The good news is that they are only dormant, not completely gone.

Humans have many additional natural senses. With some awareness and intentional practice, you can use these natural senses to make your interactions with horses better.

Below is a list of several of our other senses along with some suggestions on how you might use them around horses. Now that you know they actually exist, you can program your subconscious to make them super human!

Proprioception: The ability to detect where your body is in space.[9]

To test this sense, close your eyes and hold your hand out in front of you. Can you sense where it is? Can you still "see" it?

You can also test this sense with you and your horse. Have someone hold your horse or make sure you will be safe. While seated on your horse, can you detect where his feet are and where your body is in relation to his? If you feel safe, you can do this at a walk, trot, and canter. Again, with your eyes closed, can you detect where your horse's feet are and what your legs, seat, and hands are doing?

Shutting down one sense (sight) focuses your attention and helps heighten another sense. When you start paying attention to this sense, you'll be able to detect both your and your horse's body movements without having to close your eyes.

Thermoception: The sense of temperature.[10]

Thermoception is related to the sense of feel. It is the ability to detect if something is hot or cold. Using this sense, you can detect temperature without having to actually touch the object.

You can easily test this sense. Turn on one of your stove's burners. Move your hand toward the burner and you'll notice that you feel the heat without having to place your hand directly on the burner.

Stand next to your horse and place your hand, palm side down a few inches above his hair. Close your eyes and tell yourself that you want to feel changes in temperature. With your eyes open or closed, run your hand along his body. You may sense areas that are colder or warmer than others. Heat can be a sign of pain, injury, or energy congestion. Cold may indicate areas of poor circulation or energy blocks. A scar will block the normal flow of energy, so it usually "feels" a different temperature than the surrounding area.

Nociception: The ability to sense pain.[11]

Nerve cells detect pain and send the information to the brain for processing. People and animals process pain differently. Some are very sensitive to the slightest pain, while others seem to have a high tolerance.[12]

Some horses seem to be able to totally shut off intense pain. If your horse appears to have a high tolerance for discomfort, try out your newly rediscovered sense of thermoception. Close your eyes and tell your subconscious you want to notice areas that are sore. Use your new skill of thermoception to scan for areas of heat that might indicate trouble. Look for areas of his body where the muscles seem tense. Feel these areas with your hands to notice if the muscle feels hard, lumpy, or knotty and if there is a change in temperature.

Once you have heightened this sense, you may begin to notice or feel areas of pain in your horse or other people without even having to touch them!

Magnetoreception: The ability to sense magnetic fields.[13]

Animals have a highly developed sense of magnetoreception. Homing pigeons are such a great example. They will always fly back to their home, regardless of where they find themselves.

Other animals with heightened magnetoreception are salmon, sea turtles, lobsters, honey bees, and fruit flies.[14]

You may know people with a great sense of direction. They are probably highly tuned to the magnetic energy around them. Horses on a trail ride seem to naturally know which way to go to arrive back at the trailhead (usually much faster than they moved going up the trail!). When you begin to pay attention to this sense, you'll start to notice changes in the electromagnetic field. You may even be able to detect changes in brain and heart waves emitted by other people and animals.

Equilibrioception: The sense of balance.[15]

This sense is responsible for keeping you from falling over. Most equestrians work to improve their sense of balance when they ride. Try programming your subconscious to pay attention to your balance when riding. You may soon begin to notice when you are starting to lose balance or position. It might help you if you tend to sit more heavily on one side of your saddle. At least you might become aware of it before someone has to tell you.

Common Sense: The ability to make good decisions in practical matters.

By far, this may be the most important "sense" of all when working with horses! Being in a hurry, not paying attention to the horse, being distracted, and not noticing potentially dangerous situations has led to many horse/human accidents. Anyone who works around horses should develop common sense into a super power!

Some Additional Senses[16]

Texture	Time	Weight	Thirst
Taste	Muscle tension	Itch	Stretch (bladder,
Hunger	Feeling of pressure	Space	stomach, lungs)

You may be able to come up even more senses to add to this list. Ancient Egyptians believed that humans have 360 natural senses.[17] If this is true, try to imagine what these other senses might be. If we had access to all of them, we would be superhuman!

Today, technology is replacing our natural senses—it does the sensing for us. It's causing some of our natural senses to atrophy. Like any muscle, our other senses have become weaker from lack of exercise.

Unlike our ancestors, we no longer pay much attention to the energy field around us. We tend to only pay attention to the information we receive from our five senses. But in doing this, we miss so much.

As you practice the concepts in this book, you'll put your other senses back into training. Animals haven't lost their ability to detect changes in the energy field. Koda, my black and white paint gelding, helped me see this.

KODA

Koda was a big, handsome horse. But he was a few bales short of a full stack. When I started him, I felt like the guy in the movie *Groundhog Day*[18], doomed to relive the same day over and over. I even had a fellow trainer on speed dial to figure out a way to make progress in his training. Koda just couldn't seem to retain what he learned the previous day, no matter how slow or simple

I made the lessons. I often wondered if he had anything going on inside his head.

Koda

One day, Koda was out in a 20-acre pasture with the other horses. As I went through my daily routine, I noticed that he wasn't out grazing. Instead, he spent the day staring at one of my female llamas. This went on for hours.

Later in the day, a friend of mine stopped by to visit. We were on my front porch talking when we saw Koda run around the side of the llama pen and jump over the fence into the driveway. He headed straight toward us at a full gallop, but then performed a perfect rollback and headed back toward the llama pen.

I had three immediate thoughts: 1) Wow, he should be a reiner; 2) No wait, perhaps he should be a hunter-jumper; and 3) Oh my, there must be something wrong. He's playing Lassie!

My friend and I ran toward the pen and witnessed the llama's water break. She gave birth a few minutes later. Koda had sensed something we humans were oblivious to. This incident gave me a whole new respect for him.

Koda and his llamas.

What Koda sensed was information that exists in the energy field. He used his other senses to pick up information that "told" him that the mother llama was experiencing a profound change of some sort. I realized he had a special talent after all.

We all have special talents. We simply aren't aware of them . . . yet!

CHAPTER 7

What do you expect?

"A wonderful gift may not be wrapped as you expect."

—Jonathan Lockwood Huie

C athy, a woman in her late 40s, had loved horses since she was a child. After pleading with her parents, they agreed to let Cathy take riding lessons at a stable near their home. She was 10 years old and was living her dream. Over the next eight years, Cathy spent the weekends and summers taking riding lessons, brushing horses, braiding their manes, going on trail rides, and mucking stalls.

As much as she loved horses, Cathy left them behind when she moved to another city to attend college. Her goal was to buy a horse after she got a good job. But soon, a lucrative career, a husband, and two kids consumed all of her time. She put her dream of owning a horse on hold. When the kids left for college, Cathy had the time and money to devote to her childhood passion.

Cathy found a nationally recognized trainer who helped her buy Etoile, the 16.3 hand warmblood of her dreams. He was stunning and talented. Cathy was a dedicated and competent rider. Together, they couldn't lose. Even his name meant "star." She proclaimed to all her friends that in a year, she and Etoile would win every competition they entered.

Cathy pursued her new obsession in the same way she approached her corporate job—with the intensity of a border collie and the drive of a wall-street stockbroker. After all, she reasoned, this approach had earned her success, prestige, and money. It was her tenacity, attention to detail, and determination that had allowed her to rise to the top of her profession in a field dominated by men. It was the only model of success she knew—and she believed it worked in all areas of life. She was about to find out that this model didn't work so well with horses.

Etoile and Cathy made fantastic progress for the first nine months. Just as she predicted, they became the stars of the stable. Cathy attributed their success to her commitment to daily rides and biweekly dressage lessons coupled with her morning yoga and Pilates classes. When she had to attend out-of-town meetings, Cathy made sure her trainer rode Etoile so he wouldn't miss one precious day of work.

According to the quarterly training schedule Cathy had developed, she and Etoile were on track to achieve "their" goal right on time. Then, around month 10, something didn't seem right. Etoile, once an enthusiastic partner, seemed distant. Cathy noticed that he was turning away from her when she entered the stall to put his halter on. There was another troubling problem. Every time she mounted, the once gentle and obedient gelding would pin his ears and raise a back foot. It was as if he wanted to kick her!

Etoile's threatening gesture scared Cathy, but also made her furious. She loved him but was not about to tolerate this kind of behavior. When Etoile did this, she heard her trainers voice in her head say, "Nip it in the bud before it becomes a habit . . . you need to make sure he knows who's in charge." Cathy made sure she hit him on the flank with her dressage whip each time he threatened to lift his back leg. This became their new mounting routine.

Cathy worried about Etoile, so she had her vet, a chiropractor, an acupuncturist, and an equine nutritionist check him over. None of them found anything alarming or out of the ordinary. They all agreed that Etoile was in perfect health and a model of fitness.

In desperation, Cathy consulted a well-respected trainer who specialized in behavioral problems. He came out to evaluate Etoile and recommended some different techniques to work on the horse's "resistance" problem. He suggested longer workouts and gave Cathy some tips about how to establish more authority over Etoile. This trainer told Cathy, "You need to get a handle on this before it gets any worse. You must establish yourself as the leader in this relationship." He showed her how to command Etoile's respect. Cathy was a high-level corporate supervisor in a Fortune 500 company. She felt confident in her ability to be a strong leader for Etoile.

Armed with this new strategy, Cathy forged ahead. For a while, the techniques seemed to work like a miracle. She and Etoile were back on track! Then one day, Etoile came out of the stall a little off in his right front. Cathy rode him, and he seemed to work out of the stiffness after a few minutes of trotting. This continued for a week, and then the few minutes of trotting didn't work. He was lame.

The vet came out and ran tests, but couldn't diagnose the cause of the lameness. She suggested Cathy give Etoile a week of stall rest and she would reexamine the leg in a week. Cathy was nervous. They couldn't afford a week off. It would mean they wouldn't meet their goal for that quarter. But she loved Etoile and did as the vet recommended.

The week off did no good. The vet conducted some additional evaluations, but still couldn't find anything wrong. She suggested a longer layoff, additional tests, nutritional supplements, and some therapeutic wraps.

Cathy flew into a panic. She realized that she would never reach her goal with Etoile if he had to take any more time off. Brokenhearted, Cathy had a hard decision to make. If she kept Etoile, she would never meet her goal for the year. After thinking it over for a night, Cathy asked her trainer to look for another horse, one that would be capable of taking her to the top . . . and quickly.

Cathy found a teenage girl at the stable whose parents agreed to pay a very reduced price for Etoile. The parents knew about Etoile's condition, but thought he would be a wonderful companion for their only child Rachael. And it would give her something to think about other than boys!

When Racheal learned that she was Etoile's new owner, she wept. She couldn't believe she was now the proud owner of such a magnificent horse. Rachael spent hours brushing Etoile, telling him her secrets, braiding his mane, taking him on walks, and enjoying slow trail rides.

After a few months with his new girl, Etoile was completely sound. He never took another lame step. He never threatened to kick her when she mounted for a ride. He didn't need Rachael to show him who was boss—he willingly did anything she asked. One year later, they won their first blue ribbon together. Twenty years later, Rachael wept as she laid Etoile to rest. He was the horse of her dreams.

Cathy's trainer found her another horse. His name was Destin. He was more expensive than Etoile, but was ready for the show ring. Cathy was ecstatic. She would be on track after all. They made it halfway through their first winning show season together before Destin took his first lame step . . .

Expectations

In Cathy's case, the intensity of her energy and expectations caused problems for her horses. In her quest to reach her goals, she missed both subtle and monumental clues that her horses were headed toward injury or burnout.

Can you recall a situation similar to Cathy's? Or maybe you know of a horse pushed beyond his or her limits. Just like people, horses can burnout on their work. This often happens when the owner's expectations don't fit with the horse's abilities or personality. Talented, smart, and athletic horses are more likely to fall victim to over training and burnout. These types of horses, and those who are highly sensitive, need slow and careful handling. This helps preserve their motivation, trust, and enthusiasm for their job.

Now, think about the expectations you have for your horse. Are you able notice the subtle clues your horse gives you to let you know if you're pushing too hard or too fast? Can you identify these clues before they turn into troublesome behavioral or physical problems?

If your horse displays a behavior you interpret as resistance, it's important to ask two questions: 1) Is the resistance mental/emotional? or 2) Is the resistance physical? It can be both. Let's look at how to identify the ways your horse tries to "tell" you the reason for his resistance.

Mental resistance often occurs when the horse:

- is worked while in a flight, fright, or freeze state of mind
- is pushed too fast in his training
- has no breaks (time off) in the training or riding regiment
- doesn't understand what you're asking—the cues aren't consistent, concise, and/or clear
- doesn't have a confident rider
- has an abusive rider/trainer
- is asked to perform while in pain
- is asked to perform maneuvers beyond his physical abilities
- has no connection or communication with the rider
- has a rider whose energy is too intense
- has a rider who can't control his or her own thoughts or emotional state

Common behaviors caused by mental resistance:

- refusal to move forward
- ignoring the rider's cues
- difficulty halting or standing still
- bolting
- running off/no speed control
- shying/anxiety
- kicking
- biting
- bucking

- head tossing
- stall vices
- being barn sour
- muscle tension/stiffness
- checking out

Physical resistance can be due to:

- pain
- body stiffness
- poor shoeing/trimming
- an undiagnosed injury
- an inability to perform a physical maneuver

A horse in pain can display many of the same behaviors as one with a mental resistance. To rule out physical pain, have a professional such as a vet, chiropractor, acupuncturist, nutritionist, massage therapist, farrier, or energy worker evaluate your horse. Know what is normal for your horse so that you can notice when something is a bit "off."

Solutions

When you establish a true heart and mind connection with your horse, you'll be able to tell why he or she is displaying a particular behavior. You'll even be able to tell if the resistance is coming from a mental or physical problem you are having! Once you understand the root cause of the horse's behavior, you can take steps to remedy the problem. If you're not sure how to proceed, consult with someone who practices the principles outlined in this book. Help is out there.

Being able to understand what the horse is saying takes practice and finesse on your part. Once you know how to establish a true connection and have an energetic conversation with your horse, you'll pick up the subtle clues. You'll know if your horse is just being lazy or if the root of the resistance is a mental or physical problem. Armed with this information, you can make an informed and compassionate decision about how to fix the issue.

Flight, Fright, and Freeze in Horses

It's important to learn how to identify if a horse is in flight, fight, or freeze mode. Not paying attention to this common reason for mental resistance in horses can be dangerous. When a horse is in flight mode, he or she may race around the round pen or run around on the lunge line in an attempt to flee the human. The horse may just run until he's too tired to run anymore. Or he may go into fight mode and try to kick at or charge the human. If he becomes too tired, or he decides to just give up, he'll go into freeze mode.[1]

Look at the horse's eyes. They will tell you which of these three things are happening in his brain. A soft eye is a sign that everything is well. Pay attention to horses' eyes and what behaviors they're exhibiting. That way you will learn to identify a relaxed horse eye from a stressed one. You'll also be able to evaluate if a horse is in flight, fright, or freeze mode.

Sometimes people become mesmerized by trainers who can break a horse to ride in a few days, but a word of caution: "Training" a horse while he or she is in fight, flight, or freeze mode is a tricky thing. The fast-paced and intense energy often associated with rapid training can have negative and long-lasting effects on the horse. When the horse's brain is focused on survival, it is in a reactive mode. The horse does what it needs to do to stay safe.[2] The things he does while in survival mode may mimic the desired behavior. However, attached to the memories of how to do the maneuver is a negative emotion (fear, stress, anxiety, frustration, and the like). What fires together wires together (in the brain).[3] In the future, the maneuver or the behavior may always have a level of stress or fear "wired" to it. A similar situation, person, place, or thing can trigger the flight, fright, or freeze mode. Somewhat like post-traumatic stress in a human.

For some horses, this rapid training method appears to work because the horse is obedient. But that obedience may always have a fear of punishment attached to it. The horse goes through the motions or checks out to survive or endure the human encounter. Other horses trained this way become a ticking time bomb—you may never know when they might blow. In either case, it's hard to gain back trust or establish a deep connection with horses trained this way.

A mentally or physically tired horse does not learn well. Do you remember things when you're tired? Horses trained slowly, quietly, and gently are more likely to retain what they learn. In general, they are also the ones who will seek a deep connection with humans. Trainers who make it a priority to keep the horse in a relaxed and receptive state of mind and body often receive criticism for taking too long. But the extra time pays off in the long term.

> In relaxation, a horse's brain stays primed for learning and retention. Horses trained this way will be more trusting and willing. They will seek a deep connection with humans . . . on their own.

Horse Labels

When horses don't or can't perform up to their owner's expectations, they often receive a label. This label may brand them for life. The label usually has a story attached to it. This story explains the origin of the label.

The following are examples of horse labels—good and bad. The owner's told me the story behind the label. We uncovered the real reason the horse received that label.

THE BARN BITCH

Owner's story: Lacy always tries to bite and kick me when I saddle her. She's such a bitch!

The real story: Lacy's rib was out. She experienced a lot of pain when the owner cinched up the saddle.

THE SLOTH

Owner's story: I can't seem to get Monty to move forward unless I kick him constantly. I have had to buy some bigger spurs just so he will listen to my leg. My trainer rides him, and it's like he's a different horse.

The real story: The owner suffered from depression. Stuck in a dead-end job, she couldn't find the motivation to look for something better. Riding was her only escape from her awful situation. Her "stuckness" transferred to her horse.

RODEO MAN

Owner's story: Lucky tries to bolt and buck whenever we go out on a trail ride. I can't control him.

The real story: Riding outside the arena terrified Lucky's owner. She had only been riding a year and lacked confidence in her skills. On trail rides, she got so anxious that she held the reins tight, leaned forward, and pinched her knees into Lucky's sides. She was gripped by fear of falling off and getting hurt. Everyone at the barn pressured her to get her horse out of the arena. She always agreed to go on trail rides to prove to everyone she was a good owner and would do what was best for Lucky.

THE SHOWMAN

Owner's story: Crush loves to show off. He always performs at his best when there's a crowd around. Crush is always looking at himself in the mirrors in the arena. He can't resist a camera.

The real story: Crush enjoys his work. His owner loves to show, and Crush feels no tension or anxiety in her. Instead, he feels her joy whenever he does well at the show. She laughs when he poses for the camera. He likes the feeling, and it makes him pump himself up.

THE 4,000 PIECE HORSE PUZZLE

Owners story: Franklin is so complicated. I can't figure out why he spooks so much and why he becomes so distracted by everything in his environment.

The real story: Franklin's owner lacks confidence in her ability to handle a frightened horse. She freezes when she sees something in the environment that might spook a horse. When Franklin spooks, she becomes so scared that she disconnects from him and her own body. He just needs a confident rider. And someone who isn't always scanning the environment for horse goblins.

Human Labels

Horses aren't the only ones who receive labels. Often, we assign labels to ourselves or to other riders/trainers we know. And we create a story to back up that label. The more often we tell the story, the stronger it gets.

As is true with horses, human labels tend to stick. For example, if you have labeled yourself as a timid rider, your thoughts and emotions when you're around horses will reflect that belief.

Your thoughts and emotions create physiological changes in your body[4]—and your horse picks up on that energy.[5,6] If you want to be a confident rider, you need to change your thoughts and emotions to those that a confident rider would have.

Positive self-talk is a technique that is effective in changing a negative label, or strengthening a positive one. Self-talk is what you say to yourself—silently—in your head.[7,8]

Putting your Self-Talk to Work for You

Notice what you say to yourself when you're riding or working with your horse.

Make a list of as many of these words or phrases as you can think of.

As you write them down, label them as positive or negative. Decide if they help you or hurt you.

For those that you labeled as positive, continue using them.

For those you labeled as negative, come up with some words or phrases to replace the negative ones. For example, if you say to yourself, "I always make a mistake and forget my reining pattern," change it to "I always easily remember my reining pattern."

Practice your new positive self-talk every chance you get. Include your positive self-talk in your Productive Contemplation sessions (see Chapter 3).

Be patient because it takes time to change your subconscious self-talk patterns.

Stories

Have you ever noticed that people have a story about their life? The story explains who they are, what they do, and why they do it. Everything they do stays within the character and plot line of their story. Some people hold onto a negative story about themselves for the secondary gain or payoff. They may like the attention or sympathy they receive from others when they tell their story. The stories we create for our horses work the same way.

It's often hard to break free of the story of our life. If it's a positive story and things are going well, you may not want to change your story.

What if you don't like any aspects of your life story, or the one associated with your horse?

Create positive self-talk, practice Productive Contemplation, and incorporate the principles covered in this book. These are effective ways to create a new life script for you and your horse. If you're willing to put in the time and effort, you will see changes. If you pay attention to what your horse is telling you, you can do things to change his story too.

Creating a new story for your life is a powerful technique. This is because the human brain is wired for storytelling. Before written language, stories were the only way to pass down knowledge. Our ancestors' lives often depended on remembering the information that was in the stories! After man developed written language, people wrote down their stories. With the invention of audio and visual devices, people recorded their stories. We love stories because they help us connect to one another. They reinforce who we are and our place in the world. They help us make decisions and develop empathy for others.[9,10]

You're more likely to remember a story if it contains exciting characters, a great plot line, suspense, and surprise. The more emotions it brings up, the better the story.[11] Think about the stories you remember the most. They are the ones that engaged all of your senses and made you laugh or cry, or both.

Now that you know the importance of stories, make up a new one for you and/or your horse. If you write the story down on paper, it will make it more real. The act of writing activates more of your brain and helps you remember something.[12] As you're writing, imagine the emotions you want to feel. Make your story rich in emotions, sights, sounds, smells, tastes, and body sensations. Imagine yourself walking into that new story.

I don't remember a lot of facts from my school days. Why? Because they were just bits of information. They weren't interesting, important, or relevant—especially not to my survival! The only class I truly remember from college was taught by a Native American medicine man. There were no textbooks or tests. He started each class playing his sacred flute. Then, in his soft baritone voice, he told a myth or legend of his people. Interwoven in these stories was the history of his people. Before the beginning of each class, there was a buzz of excitement and anticipation in the room. We were all like little children, excitedly waiting for grandpa to read us a bedtime story. His stories were fables for grownups—they kept us entertained and captivated for hours. I will never forget them.

CHAPTER 8

Attitude is Everything

"Attitude is like a contagious virus. It can affect everyone around you. Decide if you want to spread an epidemic of unhappiness and negativity, or infect others with joy, love, and positivity."

—Susan D. Fay, PhD

I will never forget a virus I caught at a horse show in 2006. My friend Megan and I drove more than 16 hours to get the show grounds. Even though we were tired from our 2-day drive, we could hardly contain our excitement. We loved horse shows.

Megan and I got the horses fed, watered, and settled in for the night. After a good night's sleep, we arrived at the show grounds the next morning refreshed, energetic, and tingling with anticipation. Did I mention, we loved horse shows?

It was halfway through the morning before the virus hit us both—and hard. One moment Megan and I were laughing, the next minute every bit of energy and enthusiasm drained from our bodies. We caught a negativity virus from a rider in our group. It hit us even before we set eyes on the guy who spread it to us.

Megan and I knew that something was wrong the minute we saw the rider's face. Before he said hello, he complained to us about the weather, the long plane ride, the rude show personnel, the awful food, and how exhausted he was. He criticized us for being too slow in setting up the stalls. According to him, we hadn't put things in the right places. He couldn't find his show clothes, even though they were hanging in front of his face! Nothing was right. His face, contorted into an angry grimace, cut through our good humor.

A heavy black cloud of doom and gloom settled over us and the horses. The good feelings Megan and I had enjoyed earlier in the morning were soon a distant memory. We spent the next three days depressed and pessimistic. Unlike most shows, we didn't have fun. And neither did the horses.

On the long drive home, the doom and gloom feeling lifted. Megan and I realized that we caught something from the unhappy rider. We laughed as we named it: *The 2006 Grumpy Virus*. Both of us agreed that it was the worst virus we had ever experienced. And it lasted a full three days. I joked that maybe it was an epidemic because surely there were many other people the rider came into contact with who fell "ill" to his bad attitude. We should have called the Centers for Disease Control to quarantine this rider who spread it around!

This incident happened before I knew how people affect others with their brain and heart waves. I didn't understand how someone's negative thoughts and emotions could be spread to others through the energy field. The horses also succumbed to the virus. They had their worst show ever.

This event made an impression on me. Even now, 12 years after catching the Grumpy Virus, I can't shake the memory of what happened at that show. This is why I feel the need to stress the importance of attitude. It's something we have total control over. Attitude is a choice.

What is attitude?

A person's attitude is the way they think and feel on the inside reflected on the outside.[1] In other words, it is the heart and brain wave patterns they emit into the energy field. And it's the look on their face, their body language, what they say, the tone of their voice, how they treat others, and everything else they do.

Your attitude can become a habit.[2] It's the way you react whenever you have a certain thought or emotion. If you're not aware, you can hold onto an attitude. If it's a good attitude, figure out what thoughts and emotions created it. The same is true if you have a bad attitude—find out what triggered it. A chronic negative attitude can lead to illness or disease.[3] It can also make people—and animals—ignore or want to flee from you. For these reasons, it makes sense to pay attention to your attitude.

To change your attitude, you need to change your thoughts or emotions. If you think a different thought, you will change the emotion. If you focus on changing your emotion, your thoughts will change.[4] This is often easier said than done. It takes practice. But awareness of your attitude is an important first step. Remember, you are in control, not your thoughts or emotions!

When a person says, "I can't control myself when X, Y, or Z happens," they are lying. They may not know how to control their emotions—or they don't want to. We're all strong enough to learn how to control an emotion.[5]

If someone around you has a bad attitude, you can try to get them to change their thoughts or emotion. The best antidote for a bad attitude is a big deep breath. A good joke and laughter are also good ways to change someone stuck in a bad attitude. However, it is the other person's responsibility to notice what they are doing and how they are affecting those around them.

It's a good idea to interact with horses only when you have a positive attitude. Your horse can tell when you're angry, upset, stressed, or worried. He may mimic your attitude and respond in a dangerous or undesirable way. If I'm having a bad day and can't change my negative emotions—or the thoughts associated with them—I don't ride or handle horses. It's not fair to my horse to infect him with a bad attitude.

Imagine how many horse problems wouldn't escalate if the rider just stopped and took a deep breath. When you focus on breathing, you go from flight, fright, or freeze mode (the reactive part of your brain) back into your rational brain. Your rational brain makes good decisions; your reactive brain does not.[6]

Once, a farrier came over to trim my horses. He arrived with a bad attitude, upset about an incident that occurred at his farm the previous day. As he told me the story, I noticed that my horse became fidgety and refused to stand still. I thought it was strange because my horse was always so well-behaved. The farrier was about to hit my horse when I yelled, "Stop!" It startled him so much that he stopped mid swing. I talked with him about the sadness and frustration he was experiencing. After a few minutes, he relaxed. The horse took a deep breath, relaxed, and stood still. I also took a deep breath and relaxed.

We have all been in a situation where we experienced Human Energy Pollution. Human Energy Polluters (HEPs) emit invisible negative energy. They can often be hard to identify, especially in a group of people. We can't see the negative energy they emit, but it still affects us. Think about a time you were in a group of people and suddenly you could feel yourself begin to become anxious or agitated. Just being in the presence of a HEP can instantly change the mood of a group of people . . . for the worse. Perhaps people stopped talking. Or they became combative or argumentative. I'm not sure how to fix a HEP, but you can make sure you're not one. Being aware of, and responsible for, the energy **you** are emitting is something you have complete control over.

If you ride horses with others, pay attention to everyone's attitude. I won't get into a car with someone under the influence of drugs or alcohol. I wouldn't ride in a car with anyone who has road rage. It's far too risky. It's the same with attitude. I make it a habit not to ride horses around anyone under the influence of negative emotions or a bad attitude. It can lead to stressed horses, stressed people, and a possible accident. Remember, it's just as easy to spread a positive attitude as it is to spread a negative one.

CHAPTER 9

Trust—A Two-way Street

"Trust is the glue in life. It's the most essential ingredient in effective communication. It's the foundational principle that holds all relationships."

—Stephen R. Convey

Judy was in the stall, excitedly raking and fluffing the fresh wood shavings. She wanted it to be perfect for her new filly. Judy inhaled deeply, allowing the sweet smell of pine to permeate through her entire body. How she had missed that smell. It had been almost a year since she last bedded a big horse stall. For a moment, a wave of sadness interrupted her joy and anticipation. She recalled the warm summer night that she lost her gelding Bailey. For 30 years he was the love of her life, her best friend. Judy recalled his soft nickers as she held his head in her lap until he took his final breath. The night that Bailey left, Judy couldn't imagine ever wanting another horse. But when she saw the beautiful golden filly with the flaxen mane frolicking in a pasture not far from her home, Judy realized should could love again.

The sound of the diesel transport truck lumbering down her driveway jolted Judy back to the present. Her new 3-year-old filly Jasmine was inside. Judy anticipated that the two of them would become fast friends. But Jasmine was about to challenge everything that Judy thought she knew about creating a bond and establishing trust with a horse.

Judy prided herself on being a responsible and educated horse owner. She had spent years consuming everything natural horsemanship and was anxious to apply her expertise with Jasmine. She imagined that the natural horsemanship techniques would work faster with Jasmine than they had with Bailey. After all, the learning curve with Bailey had been slow and cumbersome. She had made mistakes with him as she struggled to master the riding and groundwork skills. But she and Bailey had persevered and eventually established a strong bond. Trust was never an issue—she trusted him and he trusted her.

With Jasmine safely in her stall and bedded down for the night, Judy felt a renewed sense of joy and purpose. It would be good to have a new life in the barn again. Her donkey Tex had become despondent after the death of his friend Bailey. But with Jasmine in the stall next to him, it seemed that life was returning to Tex as well. When he spotted Jasmine, he brayed and pranced around his pen, just like he used to do when Bailey was alive. This made Judy smile.

After giving Jasmine a few days to settle into her new surroundings, Judy decided it was time to take her to the round pen. Judy had taken lessons from the trainer who started Jasmine, so she was familiar with his methods. She was confident that in a short time, Jasmine would be following her around like a puppy. As she unsnapped the lead rope, Jasmine took off at a full gallop. She continued to run around the pen at a full speed, seemingly unaware that a human was even present. Judy applied all the techniques she knew to get Jasmine to slow down or turn. None of them worked. All she could do was wait until Jasmine was so exhausted that she stopped on her own. When this happened, Jasmine walked toward Judy and stopped. The beautiful palomino was trembling and covered in sweat.

Over the next two weeks, Judy worked Jasmine in the round pen every day. The filly became less frantic and began to listen to the commands to slow down, turn, and stop. Judy was happy that the filly was listening and obedient. The demons that possessed the golden filly that first day in the round pen appeared to be gone. But to Judy, something in Jasmine's responses seemed mechanical. This bothered her because she wanted a true relationship with her horse. She didn't want a robot.

That night, sleep didn't come easy to Judy. As she tossed and turned in bed, she came to a painful realization—maybe Jasmine would never trust her in the same way that Bailey had. After all, the techniques she was using were supposed to build trust, but they simply weren't working. She felt the warm sting of tears welling up in her eyes. She had to admit to herself that she wanted Bailey back. She cried until weariness overcame her and she feel into a deep slumber.

In her dream, Judy was a teenager again. She and Bailey were galloping across the open field behind their house. She was riding him bridleless. Tears filled her eyes, but this time they didn't sting because they were happy tears—familiar and comforting. She and Bailey were together . . .  completely. They stopped to play in the pond. Later he grazed next to her as she ate her lunch. Time seemed to stand still. It was heaven.

When Judy opened her eyes that morning, she knew what to do . . . and it was simple. She and Jasmine would play and hang out together. No rigorous training schedule and no expectations.

Judy spent the next few days simply being with her new horse. She let Jasmine free in the arena noting that the young mare seemed anxious that she may suddenly be asked to do something. But Jasmine soon relaxed. She purposely searched out Judy's company, smelling her hair and gently brushing her soft muzzle against Judy's skin.

Judy consciously sent out positive heart energy, silently acknowledging Jasmine with pictures of love and appreciation. She concentrated on her thoughts, making mind-pictures of what she intended to do prior to taking any physical action. She pictured quietly setting the saddle pad and saddle on Jasmine's back before picking up either item. She pictured Jasmine following her around the pen, comfortable and confident. With a playful attitude, she created visualizations of the two of them enjoying a relaxed hack down the horse trails.

Jasmine responded quickly, becoming calmer and much more willing to interact. She made it clear that she was enjoying Judy's company, and was open to learning new things. She no longer needed to run off nervous energy, looking to Judy for support and confidence.

By changing her own energy and expectations, in addition to being consistent in her handling and training, Judy developed a strong bond and trusting relationship with Jasmine. There were days when the two of them did nothing but hang out together in the corral or take leisurely walks with Tex. Judy didn't stop doing ground work or practicing her natural horsemanship techniques, but she kept her attitude positive and her energy playful and light. As Judy became consistent in her own energy and actions, she became a trustworthy human. Because Jasmine responded in a consistent way to Judy's energy, she became a trustworthy horse. Judy realized that maintaining trust is the responsibility of both partners in a relationship.

Jasmine and Tex

Developing Trust

Most equestrians have learned that the primary ways to develop trust with a horse is through physical interaction (e.g., grooming and handling) and conventional training, either on the ground or in the saddle. Natural horsemanship instructors stress the importance of effective ground work and moving the horse's feet as a way to establish trust and compliance. Using proper round pen methods—rather than just running them to make them tired—people can convince their horses to follow them around without a halter or lead line. Most instructors and clinicians teach students to release pressure or let the horse rest when he gives them the "correct" behavioral response. This is also touted as a good way to build trust with a horse provided you remain clear, consistent, and fair in your application of the aids.

All of these things work, but consider whether a conditioned response obtained through training methods is an indication of trust.

Is a horse following a human a sign of trust?

Perhaps, but not always. Judy would argue that a much deeper level of trust can be established when an energetic heart and mind connection is also made between a horse and a human. She discovered that it was only after she made an effort to keep her energy positive and consistent that the bond and trust between her and Jasmine began to blossom.

When you experiment with your energy around horses, it will become apparent that trust exists on many different levels. Trust between a horse and human evolves after a true heart and brain wave connection is made. When the **human** learns how to control his or her energy signature and is able to keep it positive and consistent when interacting with the horse, the horse begins to trust the human. Trust deepens further when: 1) the human is able to resist outside distractions and give the horse his or her full attention; 2) the human is reliable and dependable; and 3) the human's actions are consistent, predictable and fair.

I have always taken great care when training and interacting with my horses. I don't want to do things that would violate their trust in me. But what about horses that have been abused by humans. Can they ever trust again? It's unclear, but I believe that once trust is broken, it's hard to resurrect again. The deepest levels of trust may be difficult or impossible to attain with a severely abused horse. But there is always hope, especially if the horse is lucky enough to find a human who understands the potential for communion that exists in the energy field.

CHAPTER 10

Presence—The Colossal Superpower

"Presence is more than just being there."

—Malcolm Forbes

Have you ever been around someone who makes you feel relaxed and content, even if you're not talking or doing anything special? If so, you may have sensed you could just take a big sigh and be yourself. People like this possess the rare quality of presence. It's the ability to just BE.

> If you could develop presence, do you believe your horse would want to spend more time around you? How about other people? Do you suppose your relationship and connection with your horse and others would improve?

Horses—without human interference—have presence. They have a natural ability to just BE. If you practice the principles outlined in this book, you can cultivate this rare quality in

127

yourself. Presence is the greatest gift you can give to any person or animal. The best part of giving this gift is that it doesn't cost you anything. And you can re-gift it as many times as you like! No one will mind.

Presence is the most important thing you need to develop if you want to experience communion with your horse. It is also an essential ingredient to creating and maintaining a sacred space.

There are other definitions of presence,[1] but for our purposes, consider it a set of internal qualities that express energetically. When a person has these qualities, they create a loving and relaxed atmosphere around themselves. People who enter their space get to soak up all the wonderful feelings. There is no judgment. Everyone can be themselves.

Presence is the ability to be honestly present in the here and now—body, mind, and spirit. You can't gain presence until you're genuine. By genuine, I mean that you know yourself inside and out. And you're content with who you are. Without a protective facade or internal resistance, you become totally congruent in mind and body. You can acknowledge the positive parts and accept the negative parts. You strive to improve yourself—for you, not others. You create no smokescreens to cover up your faults. You don't pretend to be someone you're not. You simply ARE.

Four main qualities that a person has to master if they want to begin developing presence:

Positive and loving heart energy

Empathy

Genuineness/authenticity

Ability to be in the present moment

Qualities that help you develop presence into a Colossal Superpower:

- Capacity to let go of worry or anxiety
- No need to control people/horses or situations
- A positive attitude
- Emotional stability
- Listening skills
- Awareness and control of your thoughts and emotions
- Ability to stay focused on a singular thought or idea
- Inner contentment
- Non-judgmental toward others
- Absence of ego (no need to prove anything to anyone)
- Personal stability/power (no need to use others to satisfy your own unmet emotional needs)
- Self-assurance and quiet confidence
- Inner strength
- Awareness of self
- Clear and selfless intentions
- Ability to ignore outside distractions
- Desire to connect with others—heart-to-heart and mind-to-mind

This is a long list! You may assume it would take forever to cultivate these qualities in yourself. But don't fret! You can become a master of presence by focusing on the first four qualities: a loving heart, empathy for others, genuineness/authenticity, and the ability to be in the present moment.

Positive and Loving Heart Energy

When you create a positive and loving emotion in your heart, you create an amazing energy. If you imagine it extending outside yourself, and encompassing other people or horses, they get to experience it with you. They entrain to the positive heart energy waves emanating from you. When a horse senses this energy, he or she will often lick and chew, yawn, come closer, or gently touch the person creating it.

Empathy

Empathy is the ability to put yourself in someone else's shoes—or hooves. You can experience the world from their perspective. Once there, it's possible to understand their struggles. You can celebrate their accomplishments.

Empathy allows you to take a pause with your horse when things are going wrong. During this pause, you can take time to explore the reason for the problem—you can see it from the horse's point of view. It reduces misunderstanding because you can then take actions that encourage cooperation. Every person and every being want to have their "voice" heard and understood.

Genuineness

Genuineness or authenticity comes when you no longer worry about what others think of you. When you present your true self to others, the pressure of keeping up a facade will lift.

You feel free. Horses don't like people who are incongruent. They often do things to expose the "true" person behind the curtain. That's why they're so good at equine-assisted therapies— they play out a person's inner struggles, thoughts, and emotions. They're not fooled by the facade.

Being in the Present Moment

The ability to be in the present moment with your horse or a person can be challenging. There are so many distractions and things that beg for your attention. If you worry about what the horse did last week, or focus on what he might do today, you remove yourself from the present moment.

If you become distracted by thoughts, emotions, or things in your environment (e.g., cell phones, conversations with others, or watching what others are doing), you can't focus on being present with your horse. You may miss critical messages from your horse or your environment. More than once, I heard someone lament, "I should have been paying attention. I could have avoided that accident."

Being present is also about letting someone or something know that you care. If you're always distant, distracted, or focused on someone or something else, you will have a hard time forming a strong bond with your horse or people. It's hard to convince someone you care when you never give them your full attention.

I've witnessed equestrians transform their relationship with their horse by taking these four steps to developing presence. By just focusing on creating a positive and loving heart energy, developing empathy for their horse, noticing times they're not their authentic self, and removing distractions, their horse became calmer and more relaxed. They became more horse-like. They were meeting their horse at a common place—a place where communion happens.

Awareness

At the root of developing presence is the ability to be aware. Presence requires both internal and external awareness skills. In several chapters in this book, you have learned many of the skills needed to develop presence.

The path to having presence may resemble mindfulness practices. However, the focus of mindfulness is to gain awareness of **your** emotions, thoughts, and bodily sensations and what is occurring around **you**. It's all about **you**.[2]

Inner awareness is the focus of mindfulness. When we work with horses, inner awareness is important, but external awareness of others is also important. We need to be tuned in to our horse, cognizant of what's happening around us, and alert to changes in our environment. When we are aware, both externally and internally, we pick up subtle energy clues that keep us safe and help us enjoy the time we spend with our horse.

As you push yourself to go beyond this concept of mindfulness to include your horse, other people, and your environment, you'll begin to understand how your thoughts, emotions, and attitude affect others. It's important to always keep in mind that you're responsible for the energy you are putting out into the world.

As humans, we often get stuck in routines. We go about each day doing the same things in the same way. When something becomes a routine, we stop paying attention to the world around us. And we become so inner focused that we can't see anything beyond a small area right in front of our face. Even then, we might not notice the details. We lose our peripheral vision, we have only superficial contact with others, and we can't connect with information available to us in the energy field. We do many things at once, but we do none of them well.

There are people who take great pride in their ability to multitask. It is their super power. They say that they can text, email, tweet, and talk on their cell phone when they're at work and when they're interacting with other people or their horse. A great deal of research has recently been done on this topic. Neuroscientists have revealed that multitasking is a myth. Multitasking is not the same as multi-focused. Your conscious brain can't pay full attention to two or more different tasks at once. You can still do several tasks at the same time, but you won't do any of them as well as you could if they each had your individual focus.[3]

Learning how to be present and fully aware takes practice and intention. If you want to develop greater internal and external awareness, you can program your brain to become a better observer. Just like developing your other senses, close your eyes and tell yourself, "I will see any small change in my surroundings." You can be more specific and decide what small change you want to recognize. Maybe it's a tense muscle in your horse, or a gopher hole out on the trail. Just let your subconscious go to work scanning the environment and it will bring these small things to your conscious awareness.

It takes energy to keep your brain focused. Distractions are a way to avoid dealing with your own thoughts and emotions.[4] Our brains also like stimulation, especially external stimulation.[5] We don't like to work hard to stimulate our brain—we want it done for us. It's easier to watch a movie than use our imagination to dream up a story.

Many of us have forgotten how to stimulate our own brains without technology and without using someone or something to fill the silent void. But we only learn who we are and what we can do if we spend time in the quiet place within ourselves. It's the place where creativity blossoms and all our senses heighten. When we become comfortable there, it becomes the place where communion with another being is possible.

CHAPTER 11

The Lost Art of Conversation

"A conversation is so much more than words: A conversation is eyes, smiles, the silences between the words."[1]

—Annika Thor

Conversations that include moments of silence are rare, especially when more than two people are involved. When they happen, each person leaves with a warm feeling that is hard to forget. One such conversation stands out for me.

I was on vacation with my sister in South Dakota. We stopped by to visit with two of my sister's friends on the reservation, a Lakota Sioux tribal elder and a medicine man. I can't remember what we talked about, but there was a natural and easy flow to the conversation. Each person spoke while the others listened. There were lovely natural pauses in the conversation that no one needed to fill with words. The pauses felt like they were actually a necessary part of the conversation. Each person showed respect for the other. There were no interruptions or people talking over each other. We laughed. We shared sad and happy stories. We truly connected. That deep, heart-felt communion is what I'll never forget. I would love to relive that experience.

135

What if your horse couldn't wait to experience that type of conversation with you? Wouldn't it be great if you left your horse wanting more of you? You can. All you have to do is throw out the rules and habits of conversation that apply in the human world and become more horse-like.

I felt driven to discuss this concept with the participants at a clinic I was holding at a gorgeous Colorado ranch. I thought that the lunch break would be a great time to bring up the subject. Everyone grabbed their food and sat down at the large dining table in the house. The table was situated next to a massive picture window. The first thing to catch my eye was the spectacular view of the distant snow-capped mountain range. The vistas were breathtaking. Catching the sudden flick of a tail, my eyes were drawn to a small herd of horses in the corral below.

I directed everyone's attention to them. They appeared so content, standing nose to nose, heads lowered, with half-closed eyes, and a rear foot cocked. They were enjoying each other's company and happy to do nothing. It was the perfect example of presence, of horses simply *being*. No agenda, no stress, just quiet connection and silent communication. Communion.

The chatter in the room stopped as each participant gazed at the herd. The energy of the room shifted. We all experienced a beautiful and soul enriching *pause.*

Human-Equine Communication

The questions on the minds of many equestrians are:

How do we (humans) learn to consciously communicate more effectively with horses?

How do we develop a common language so that we can actually have a conversation our horse wants to be a part of?

To answer these questions, let's first look at how horses and humans communicate with members of their own species.

Some of the ways that humans communicate with each other is through language, voice tone and pitch (from whispers to yelling), technology, writing, drawing, body posture, facial gestures, touch, eye contact, humor, music, and hand gestures.[2] Even with the myriad of sophisticated communication methods available to them, humans still experience many misunderstandings with each other.

When we observe horses, we see that they communicate with each other using their ears, eyes, certain vocal sounds, touch, and body movements/posture.[3,4] Compared to humans, horses appear to have far fewer and less complex communication tools available to them. But somehow, their communication with each other is clear and concise—and there are few misunderstandings. Why?

Before answering this question, let's look at how humans generally try to communicate with horses. We use our voice, seat, legs, body posture, weight, and pressure (touch), along with a variety of aids such as reins, spurs, whips, and bits. Even with all these communication tools, along with training advice and expertise available to us, we often struggle to convey our intentions to our horses. Miscommunications and misunderstandings between horses and humans are common and often difficult to fix.

Perhaps, if we look at more subtle ways that horses transmit and receive information from their environment, we could learn to communicate with horses and other humans better. Consider the idea that horses have complex conversations with each other—and us—using the energy field. They send energetic pictures, intentions (thoughts and ideas), and emotions. They also "read" the physiological changes in other beings (e.g., heart rate, respiration, and galvanic skin response). They feel or sense heart and brain waves. They "see" the energy frequencies of objects in their environment, perhaps with their eyes, or possibly with senses humans don't possess, and therefore don't recognize or understand.

Horses' ability to send and receive energetic information is quite sophisticated, much more so than that of humans. This energetic information is fast, clear, concise, and understandable. So, when I said we should become more horse-like, I mean that we should learn to connect to and use the tools of communication that are available to us in the energy field. Horses can be **our** linguistic teachers because they are already quite adept at speaking and understanding the universal language of energy.

HEATHER AND MIA

Heather came to my clinic with two horses. On the first day, we worked with her off-the-track thoroughbred, focusing on strengthening the connection and helping Heather become more focused. Heather said she was easily distracted, and so we did a short hypnosis session so that she could block out some of the outside noises that kept calling for her attention. After that,

Heather was able to become more present with her horse and the session went well.

On the second day of the clinic, Heather wanted to work with her mare Mia. She told me that Mia was very obedient, but there was no real connection between them. In our session, she wanted to do the same thing we had done the previous day with her thoroughbred. But she said with a sigh, "Mia is going to be really tough because she doesn't care to connect."

Inside, I panicked for a moment because I wasn't sure what would happen, if anything. To make matters worse, we were in a big round pen, and there were several geldings around the outside. Mia was in heat and intent on hanging out with the geldings. She showed no interest in us whatsoever. Someone asked if they should catch the geldings and put them away, but I said no. We were working on distractions the previous day. This was just going to be another distraction. A colossal one!

Heather and I hung out on the other side of the round pen from Mia. I guided Heather through the body scan and heart energy exercises (see Chapter12). We did them together. We worked again on her focus and making mental pictures. She was telling me how much she wanted a true heart connection with Mia. Just as she got the words out, Mia turned and walked toward us with a direct, purposeful stride. She walked right up to Sally and placed her forehead on Heather's chest. It took my breath away. Heather was speechless. Little did I know, that was just the beginning.

Mia only stayed with us for a moment before she walked off, stopping about 20 feet away. Mia stood for a minute, circled around a few times, and laid down. I had never had this happen in a clinic before. At first, I thought maybe Mia was sick because her legs got really stiff. Then she sighed, relaxed, and laid her head on the ground.

Heather and I watched Mia for a few minutes, confused by her behavior. Finally, Heather asked me what she should do.

Truthfully, at that moment, I wasn't sure. I suggested she could walk up and pet Mia on the neck. Heather said that in the past, she had tried to pet Mia when she was laying down, but she always got up. She decided to give it a try anyway. As Heather walked toward Mia, the mare didn't move. Nor did she try to get up when Heather knelt on the ground next to her head. Heather sat on the ground stroking Mia's head and neck for a long time. The glow on her beaming face said it all. We were both experiencing something truly unexpected and remarkable.

After a few minutes, Heather got on her feet and walked toward me, awe struck. In hushed words we talked about what happened—that Mia had offered the gift of pure trust and connection. As we were talking, Mia got up and went back over to the geldings. However, she didn't stay long before she walked back to where we were standing. As Heather and I continued to talk, Mia put her head down low, cocked a back foot, and closed her lovely brown eyes. Heather was relaxed, focused and present. We had truly become more horse-like in our energy. Mia had chosen, on her own, to stay with us in the sacred space we had created.

Connecting and Communicating with your Horse

The things you currently do to communicate with your horse are valid and not to be discarded. You'll still use the aids you're used to, but now you'll incorporate some of the invisible aids available to you in the energy field. When you become good at accessing these new aids, your interactions with your horse will become easier and more fluid. Your horse will become more relaxed and willing. Fewer miscommunications will occur.

In Chapter 4, you learned how to use mental imagery to improve your riding. Mental imagery is a way to "speak" to your horse using pictures. You send your mind pictures out as energy waves and your horse picks them up and interprets them. Think of yourself as the TV station that broadcasts a program over the air waves. Your horse's brain and body are the TV set that tunes into your program. Imagine broadcasting something that is interesting and meaningful to your horse and he will want to tune into your station! When I started making clear pictures, and added emotions (the sound), and intentions (the genre or topic) when interacting with horses, the changes in my horses were amazing.

University professor and autistic advocate Temple Grandin contends that autistic people are more like horses—they "see" the world as mental images.[5] I had an opportunity to experiment with this theory. I was at my friend's house and her autistic grandson was visiting. He was running around, seemingly in his own world. He was about three years old and didn't speak yet. I started sending him love energy from my heart, and I made some pictures in my mind. As he was running past me, he stopped, looked at me and placed his little hand on my cheek. His grandmother about fell out of her chair. She said that she had never seen him do anything like that before. Perhaps it was his way of acknowledging the love story I broadcast to him through the energy field!

The first step in having a conversation is establishing a connection.[6] How to go about this with your horse has been presented in the previous chapters. You can also refer to Chapter 12, for an overview of the process. Once you have established the connection, you'll want to start the conversation. The ability to have an ongoing, two-way conversation with a horse is a dream of many equestrians.

When having a conversation with a horse, make very clear pictures of what you want your horse to do. Include how you want the maneuver to look and feel—for both you and your horse. Maintain a positive emotion, and try not to let anything he does frustrate you or make you mad. When I do this, I'm careful not to picture what I DON'T want. The ability to make clear and vivid images and create the feeling you are striving for helps your horse understand. If you're consistent, before long your horse may even begin to do what you want automatically, just from you thinking about it.

How to Start a Conversation with your Horse

Keep a single thought streaming in your mind and imagine it's like a movie that runs just a few seconds in front of actual time.

Add a positive emotion such as joy, love, or contentment. Feel that emotion in your heart and try to keep it going.

Allow your face to gently smile.

Slow your breathing rate.

Think about the heart and brain waves that you're producing.

Imagine a bubble of positive energy around you—one your horse wants to connect with because it's loving, nurturing, steady, and predictable.

Example of how a conversation with your horse might go in your head:

"Hey, let's do this. Are you ready? Yes! You've got it! That's what I wanted." Pause and just ride and listen with your body and your mind to the horse. Then, make images in your mind of what you want the horse to do. "Ok, now let's go do that and watch where your feet are. No, not quite. Yes, that's it! Good Boy!" Pause. Listen to the horse's body with your instincts and your heart. Feel if his body is tense or relaxed. Give him time to think and process the messages you are sending. Notice any resistance.

SARA

I was lucky enough to have a horse who worked almost entirely off of my thoughts and pictures. Sara was one of the first foals I bred. I was there when she was born. Of all my horses, she was by far the smartest—and one of the hardest to start. When I tried to begin her initial training at three, she was a maniac. Unfocused and over-reactive, I decided I wasn't making any real progress. I got the feeling she just wasn't quite ready for school, so I turned her out with the broodmares for another year.

The next year, Sara was the star student. Everything I thought she didn't learn before was there and her training progressed quickly and easily. I had a hard time believing she was the same horse. Before long she was my favorite horse to ride. All I had to do was think something and make a picture of it. She responded immediately, and did whatever maneuver I held in my mind.

Sara showed me how sensitive horses are to mental pictures and human brain and heart waves. Humans understand images and emotions—so do horses. This is not anthropomorphizing, it has been documented by researchers[7,8,9]. Even if you don't believe that horses see your mind pictures, understand that they are sensitive enough to detect the physiological changes in your body when you have different thoughts and emotions. Just experiment with these concepts to begin the process of constructing a universal language with your horse. Remember to stay physically, mentally, and emotionally relaxed—thinking takes you out of the place where true communication happens.

Sara

You now have an idea of the basic steps needed to begin having a conversation with your horse. Don't be discouraged if at first, your horse chooses not to join this conversation. It may be because he has been formally operating under Option #1 (ignore the rider) that I talked about in Chapter 3. If you have a habit of riding with racing thoughts or while you are experiencing an emotional upheaval, your horse may not initially believe that the "new" you can be trusted. Or he has gotten used to tuning you out. With consistency, you'll prove to him that you're different, interesting, and trustworthy.

Often horses tune out humans because there are so many thoughts going through the riders' head at any one time, the horse is left to guess which one is important. If he chose to follow the wrong one often enough—and got in trouble for it—he probably made a decision that it was safer to just ignore you.

Ask yourself, "What would my horse see if he looked inside my head? Would it be a tornado of thoughts or a gentle breeze?"

It is vital to remember that horses pick up images we make in our minds, and the changes in our physiology that go along with them. If you're thinking, "I don't want him to bolt out the gate—he always tries to do that," be aware that the picture you just made in your mind looks like your horse bolting out of the gate. And you probably attached a negative emotion like fear or anger to the picture. And your muscles got tense and your breathing changed. The horse interpreted your physiology and picture as, "She wants me to try to bolt out the gate. I will because she's afraid, so there must be something dangerous in the arena. I'm a good and obedient horse, so I'll do it for her."

This does not mean that you're to side with the horse every time he or she does something naughty. But remember, they're communicating with the energy field and trying to interpret the images in your head. If you're interested in changing an un-wanted habit in the horse, it's important to be very clear in your own mind so that he can learn what you expect of him.

Many good horses receive a bad label because of previous be-haviors. Once labeled, the horse lives up to expectations. If it's a positive label, that's great. If it's a negative one, it could mean a lifetime of different owners and continual unwanted behaviors from the horse. That's because each person who hears the story of the horse's past makes pictures of it in their mind and trans-mits the picture and feelings back to the horse. He can't move beyond the movie about his life. He has been typecast into a role he may or may not want to play. He becomes conditioned to the point that his behaviors become part of his personality. This hap-pens with people too—they tend to live up to or down to the story they, or someone else, created about them.

How to Make a TV Movie for Your Horse

Make clear pictures of what you **want**, not what you don't want.

Maintain a singular thought stream in your mind.

Maintain a neutral or positive emotion (keep your body relaxed and don't get rattled).

Keep a soft, but firm intention.

Believe, without a doubt, that he can hear you and see the mental pictures you make in your head.

Have faith that he will do it right.

Pause and praise him for the desired behavior.

Types of Conversations

Informational Conversation

1a) Drill Sergeant: One-way, no heart

If you think of a Drill Sergeant, he just gives commands and expects immediate obedience in the form of a "Yes Sir!" The Drill Sergeant barks out orders and commands and displays no empathy. In this "conversation," one person talks **at** the other. The other person's response or feelings are not important to the conversation. The Drill Sergeant may get respect, but no one wants to spend time with him or her.

Examples:

- Horse trainers with an agenda and time constraints.
- Boss who treats employees like robots.
- A speaker who doesn't connect with his or her audience and fails to ignite listeners to take action.
- Egotistical person who talks over others and never listens.

1b) Parent: One-way with heart

In this type of conversation, a parent or caregiver may say, "Don't touch that, it could burn you." The child reacts by changing his or her behavior. No verbal response is expected from the child. This is similar to a Drill Sergeant because obedience is expected, but the message is delivered with love, kindness, and empathy.

Examples:

- Horse trainer or rider who loves his horse but doesn't believe or know how to establish a two-way conversation.
- Speech that moves people. The audience is left feeling like the speaker was talking directly to them.

Pseudo Conversations

Talking Conversation: Two-way, no heart

This is a type of "conversation" that just involves the exchange of words between two or more people. No true connection occurs, nor is it wanted. Many of the conversations we have fall into this category.

In Pseudo Conversations, both parties are not particularly interested in the other. Conversations are superficial and may leave one or more people feeling that they weren't heard or acknowledged. Often these conversations turn into a type of competition to see who can talk the most, the loudest, or get the last word in.

A Pseudo Conversation is used to pass time or fill an unmet need for attention, recognition, or esteem. Generally, these conversations have no pauses because each moment is filled with words. They can also become quite loud because people feel the need to talk over each other to be heard. Pauses are immediately filled with more words.

Examples:

- Boss to employees in business meeting.
- Email and text exchanges.
- Riders with a need to meet their own goals or agenda.
- Riders with racing thoughts or uncontrolled emotions.
- Horses who "talk back" to the rider using unwanted behaviors.

Genuine Conversation

Loving Conversation: Two-way, with heart (heart-to-heart)

Each person is allowed to talk and have their voice heard. There are natural pauses because people are thinking about what the other person said. There's an underlying heart emotion of love, genuine caring, and empathy for the other person. Each person feels good after the interaction and leaves wanting to spend more time communicating.

True connection occurs because each person feels that the other understands them. One person listens while the other is talking. The listener is not busy formulating the next response or topic. The conversation has a natural and comfortable flow.

Some public speakers actually leave you with the feeling that they had a conversation with YOU. This is because they have included heart love in their talk. They have a desire to help people. Passion and love emanates from their heart. You feel good because you have entrained to their strong heart energy.

> The way you feel **after** a conversation will tell you whether it was delivered with heart or without. Think about your own conversations and ask yourself the following questions:
>
> - Which category would you assign most of your human-to-human conversations to?
>
> - Which category would you assign most of your human-to-horse conversations to?
>
> - How do your conversations differ depending on what setting you're in?
>
> - Do they differ depending on whether you are with family, friends, children, business associates, horses, or pets?
>
> - What category does texting or email fall into?
>
> - Do emojis actually add genuine emotion?

The Art of the Pause

You've probably watched a rider who continually asks the horse to do something—soften here, yield there. They deliver a non-stop barrage of orders that are expected to be obeyed or some type of punishment will follow—a jerk of the rein, a spur in the side, or a hit with the whip. This is the Drill Sergeant in all his or her glory. There are no pauses until the horse is returned to the stall or corral. It's hard to imagine that a horse treated this way is enthusiastic about spending time with a human.

Endless trips around the round pen and wet saddle blankets are just another form of one-way conversation, but sometimes there is a pause. The pause is inserted after the horse performs the desired action. This is a reward/punishment type of conversation. As long as you do what I ask, I'll give you a little break. The conversation is still one-way. There may be connection with heart, but no real conversation happens.

> What if the trainer paused after showing the horse something and waited for a response? What if the trainer asked the horse: "How can I explain it better?" "Did, you get it?" and "What do you need help with?"

The pause allows time for the brain to relax and process information. It also allows time for the horse to "say" something in response. He feels like he's a part of the conversation. He has a chance to tell you if he's fearful, anxious, or enthusiastic. You give him an opportunity to connect to you. The pause is the invitation for conversation to begin. It's a chance to quiet your own mind and stop talking so that you can listen and begin to hear the subtle whisper of your horse's "voice." It may appear as a flash of an image, a thought, an idea, a feeling, a word, or a knowing. When you acknowledge the message and send an energetic response back to your horse, you feel his body relax. He may lick, chew, yawn, lower his head, and/or soften his eye. If he does, you know he got the message. He joined the conversation.

By incorporating the pause into your training or interactions with your horse, it will allow information from the energy field to enter into the conversation. It was always there—you just never stopped long enough or were quiet long enough to hear it or let it speak.

If you put away your technology (e.g., cell phone, iPod, or ear buds) and listen, you're more likely to hear an energy whisper. Technology helps us connect on a superficial level, but it doesn't contain heart, emotion, empathy, and spirit. It also distracts us and keeps us from being totally present with another. Being totally present is a requirement for deep and meaningful connection and conversation. It is also essential if you want to create a sacred space where you can experience communion with your horse or another person.

Leadership?

You need to be a leader for your horse.

This is now the catch phrase clinicians and riding instructors use to describe the type of relationship/conversation you should have with a horse.[10] It's not a bad concept, and is certainly much better than the outdated Drill Sergeant relationship that required you to show your horse who's boss. There is one problem though—no one seems to agree on what being a leader really means.

There have been many different "leaders" in human history. They all had followers, but their methods and motivations were quite different. Adolph Hitler used propaganda, cruel tactics, and intimidation to persuade people to adopt his agenda.[11] Martin Luther King used his voice to inspire others to march and take a stand for human equality.[12] Mahatma Gandhi led by quiet example.[13] Each of these leaders had a huge following. They led people to adopt new ways of thinking and doing. But which of these leadership styles are clinicians talking about using when it comes to our horses?

> Leadership is just a word. Not only that, it's a word that people have a hard time defining. Many confuse leadership with dominance. They are NOT the same thing. When asked to describe what being a leader means, every one of my students comes up with a different interpretation.

Keep in mind that horses have no use for words. They only react to who you are in the moment. When mutual respect exists between two individuals, whether they are human-human or horse-human, the need to define leadership, or establish leadership, is often unnecessary. Let me give you an example.

CRUSH

My first foal was Crescendo, or Crush for short. He was a jet-black Morgan with a thick wavy mane and tail. He was silly and mischievous, but only around other horses. When we did things together, he was serious and solid as a rock. At shows, the things that made other horses spook, he handled with courage and grace. Once he stood stock still when we were engulfed in a huge dust devil at a show. He didn't spook when a bear walked across the trail right in front of us. At a dressage show, he trotted over a 6-foot bull snake that had slithered into the arena. Most of the time when I rode Crush, I made the decisions. One time, I had to turn the "reins" over to him. Completely.

It was the summer of 2006. My friends from Florida were visiting and we decided to go on a trail ride through Flat Tops Wilderness in Colorado. At 10,000 feet in elevation, the weather can often be unpredictable. We had left early in the morning because it was important to get back before the afternoon storms rolled in.

Flat Tops Wilderness in Colorado

Unfortunately, the storms came early that day. On our way back to the trailhead, the clouds suddenly let loose. The trail turned slick, muddy, and treacherous. The horses were having a hard time trying to make their way back up the steep and slippery trail with riders on their back. We all got off. I told Crush to find a way to get us out. I held onto the stirrup as he made his way off the trail and up a steep hill. I had handed over leadership to him. He led the entire group to safety.

Respect

When interacting with horses, don't spend precious brain energy wondering how you can be a better leader. Instead, strive to be someone your horse respects and wants to be with. This means you're predictable, consistent, congruent, fair, and fun to be around. And you have a clear intention of what you want him to do. Of course, you must maintain safe boundaries, which at times might look like dominance or even aggression, but your attitude should always be one of soft strength. Just like the athlete who tightens his core while maintaining relaxed limbs ready to complete the next feat, do your best to stay strong and centered on the inside while remaining soft and light on the outside.

Developing Soft Strength

Maintain your integrity, focus, and intent.

Remain strong inside, controlling negative thoughts and emotions.

Make clear pictures of what you want.

Stay in the present.

Have confidence in your horse-handling skills.

Don't push yourself or your horse past your capabilities. (Avoid putting either of you in dangerous situations.)

FANNY

While writing this section, I couldn't stop thinking about my horse Fanny. Fanny "raised" Crush. He was her first foal, and she did an outstanding job. I make every attempt to be like her, not only in my interactions with horses, but in my interactions with people. Even though she wasn't the leader of the broodmare band, she was the one they looked to for support and guidance.

Fyste (pronounced Feisty) was, without a doubt, the leader of my broodmares. Fyste ate first. She kicked first and asked questions later. Fyste lived up to her name. The other mares and foals stayed away from her. They all did what she wanted—and quickly. There was no question about her status as the Alpha mare. But none of the other mares or foals liked her. In fact, they usually keep their distance—she was both a leader and an outcast.

Fanny and Crush

Often, when watching the broodmares and foals in the pasture, I noticed that they hung around with Fanny. Interestingly enough, even though she was quiet and laid back, none of the horses took advantage of her. If a rowdy foal tried to show dominance around her, Fanny would just pin an ear or toss her head. The foal would immediately stop—without question and without any drama. Fanny was the nanny to the foals, and sister to the other mares. And as the designated nanny, she would watch over the foals while the other mares grazed. They trusted and respected her. But she wasn't the Alpha. She was more of a passive leader. To this day, I often hear that voice in my head ask, "What would Fanny do?"

As I reflect on the concept of leadership and horses, I think about parents and children. My father and brother teach parents how to raise responsible children.[14] I believe this is the same philosophy that I used when training my young horses. (Maybe it was Fanny's influence too.) I wanted them to grow up and be well-rounded, respectful, happy, and kind. I focused on making sure they had a good work ethic and positive attitude. I trained them to respect others' boundaries and I set the example of how to act and interact with others. By practicing the concepts presented in this book, I hoped to increase the odds that my horses would have happy owners and a good life.

When training my young horses, I always focused on creating a strong foundation, taking time to nurture a strong relationship and trust between us. I never even thought about whether I was their leader. I just practiced and modeled Fanny's methods. As a result, my young horses respected me, took care of me, and liked to be with me.

I'm so thankful for Fanny's guidance and training philosophy. I know it works and is probably the reason I was not seriously injured the first time I cantered Tank. Everything was going great during the ride . . . until he tripped. In the seconds I had to react, I knew there was no way I could pull his head up to avoid a fall. Frightening scenes played out in slow motion in my brain as I imagined my trip to the hospital—if I survived. I wondered what Tank would do when I hit the ground. My last thought was to tuck and roll. I ended up doing a graceful front flip off Tank. I landed on my feet, still holding the reins. Tank scrambled back on his feet and just stood there, as if it was all a new type of dismount. He didn't run off or look the least bit concerned. My instructor said he had deftly and intentionally stepped to the side, as if he was doing his best not to fall on top of me. She was amazed that he didn't run off bucking. I'd like to believe that Tank took care of me that day—because I raised a good citizen.

CHAPTER 12

Connecting the Pieces

". . .then it hits me. Maybe we're the pieces, What?"

—Tikkun Olam

Y ou're now familiar with the individual things you can do to enhance connection and communication with your horse. But how do you put all these pieces together? How do you create a sacred space where communion is possible? In this chapter, you'll discover a way to access all of your inner talents and start putting them to work to do just that. The examples will help you see how I do it, but keep in mind that these are merely guidelines. Experiment and have fun. Always use the most important sense of all—common sense—in all your interactions with horses. If something doesn't feel right, don't do it.

Continue to work on your horse riding and handling skills. As you begin to incorporate each of the human skills into your routine, everything you currently do with your horse will become easier and better.

You don't have to perfect each skill before it starts to work. Each of the concepts can work independent of the others. And

157

they work regardless of whether you apply them to horses, humans, or other animals.

Relaxation is the key to making everything work. Classical dressage trainers focus on rhythm and relaxation with young and old horses alike. If something begins to go wrong in a training session, they go back to establishing rhythm and relaxation.

A horse who is relaxed in his or her mind and body can:

Learn and retain information better — The brain is focused on learning rather than survival.[1,2]

The horse's muscles remain supple. They are able to produce maximum power.[3]

Rhythm creates relaxation. Relaxation fosters rhythm.[4]

Creating a Sacred Space

I do this before any interaction with my horses. After you get the routine down, it only takes a few minutes to create an intention and prepare yourself for the time you're going to spend with your horse.

GROUND YOURSELF

1. Close your eyes and take three to five slow deep breaths.

Note: Place your hand on your stomach and feel your hand rise with each inhalation. Make sure you are not shallow breathing. If your shoulders rise when you inhale, then you are shallow breathing.

2. As you continue to breath normally, place your attention on the top of your head. Imagine a positive emotion you want to have during the time with your horse. It could be something like joy, gratitude, playfulness, or love.

3. Imagine that positive emotion is contained in a beam of light or a cloud above your head. The light can be any color you choose.

4. Now, imagine you have a door at the top of your head. Open that door and let the light come in.

5. With each breath in, feel the light enter into your head and wash down through your entire body.

6. As the light moves down through your body, imagine that it takes with it any unwanted thoughts or emotions.

7. With each breath out, imagine the light takes those unwanted thoughts and emotions down through your body and out your feet, deep into the earth.

8. Imagine that your feet sprout roots, and send those roots down into the center of the earth.

BODY SCAN

1. As you continue to breathe normally, place your attention on different parts of your body, one at a time. You may want to start at your head and move down your body.

2. As your place your attention a particular area, notice if that area has any pain, discomfort, stiffness, or tension. Also, notice if you have a negative thought or emotion enter your mind.

3. If there is discomfort and pain due to a negative thought or emotion, ask if it has a message for you. The message might come as a whisper, so stay quiet and wait. If you don't get anything, that's ok. If you do, note the message and say, "Thank you."

4.   Now, just imagine the light washing the pain, discomfort, or negative thought/emotion down your legs and into the ground.

5.   You can also do a body scan on your horse at this time, or you can wait until just before you interact with him or her.

SETTING THE INTENTION

1.   With your eyes still closed, imagine how you would like your session to go. This is your intention.

For example, I like to imagine that I create a sacred space for my horse (and any other horses and riders) to be in. Imagine the space is safe and that you and your horse will have a relaxing time together. Give gratitude for the time you spend together. I make an intention that my horse and I will feel better after we're done than when we started.

2.   Imagine that the light that cleansed your body now cleanses anything negative out of the space and replaces it with something like peace, serenity, gratitude, or love.

Note:

Any time you clear out something, make sure you replace it with what you want. Otherwise, that void can be replaced by something you might not want.

CHECKING YOUR HEART ENERGY FIELD

1.   As you continue to breathe normally, place your attention on your heart.

2.   Imagine a positive emotion like joy, gratitude, or love attached to your breath.

3.   Feel the positive emotion enter your heart with each breath in.

4.   Feel it surround you with each breath out.

5.   Feel your body and mind relax.

6.   Now pretend that your breath, with the positive emotion attached to it, creates a big bubble around you.

7.   Make the bubble large enough to include your horse and the entire area where you'll be interacting with your horse.

CHECKING YOUR BRAIN ENERGY FIELD

1.   With your eyes open or closed, place your attention on your thoughts.

2.   Notice if you have scattered or racing thoughts or you're worried about something.

3.   Imagine the light washing those thoughts away, down into the ground.

4.   Notice your overall emotional state or attitude.

5.   If you still have a negative emotion, acknowledge it, receive the message, and try washing it away with the light.

6.   Place your mind on what you're doing. Brushing your horse or mucking a stall can help you get in the present moment. Doing a quick mental imagery can also help.

Notes:

You can't be present with your horse when your mind is distracted or you're highly emotional. If you can't quiet your mind and emotions, it's a good idea not to be around a horse. Your anxiety will negatively affect your horse—and other people and their horses. Find some other activity to do that will help you relax. For example, you can spend time in Productive Contemplation.

Most of the time after you have gone through the grounding, intention, and body scan process, your mind will quiet and you'll be focused on the present moment.

HONING YOUR SENSES

1. Take some deep breaths and quiet your mind.
2. Go through the grounding exercise.
3. Instead of doing a body scan, imagine relaxing each part of your body. As you do, imagine a healing light flowing through your body and removing any tension or anxiety.
4. Replace the tension with a positive feeling such as relaxation.
5. Once you are relaxed, place your focus on one of the senses you would like to make sharper.
6. Imagine how you would use your new and improved sense.
7. Tell yourself that you will notice and pay attention to the information that sense brings to you.

OPENING YOUR INTUITION

1. Practice the grounding and relaxation methods.
2. Practice some type of meditation or mindfulness method that will allow you to quiet your mind.
3. If you prefer, you can listen to a relaxation, guided meditation, and/or self-hypnosis recording. There are many available on the Internet.
4. The key to increasing your intuition is to notice what brain wave state you're in. Review the information in Chapter 2 about brain waves.
5. For now, if you can focus on trying to slow your predominate brain waves down to at least low Alpha, you will have greater access to your intuition.
6. When you can achieve a relaxed state of mind and body, imagine that you can access the energy field around you.

7. If you're highly auditory (hearing oriented), you could try what I do. Imagine that you have an old-time radio with a round dial. Turn the knob until you can tune into a particular station. If it's a person or animal you want to connect with, put their image in your mind. Then, imagine turning the dial until you no longer get static and you tune into their particular frequency or "station."

8. If you're highly visual, you might want to imagine a movie, TV, or computer screen in front of you. Focus on a certain thing you want to know more about and see what shows up on the screen.

Notes:

People receive intuitive information in different ways. When you quiet your mind, it might come as just a knowing, or maybe a bodily feeling, a quick flash of a picture, a single word, or a sound. Don't start trying to analyze with your conscious mind how it should come to you. That puts you in a Beta brainwave pattern that immediately shuts off your intuition.

Approach intuition with an open mind and playful attitude. Experiment. Take some classes. The techniques that you can use to open your intuitive channels are numerous.

The key is to create a quiet place. Intuition resides in the quiet place. It also requires you to let go of your assumptions and your need for control.

PRODUCTIVE CONTEMPLATION (PC) AND MENTAL IMAGERY—THE DYNAMIC DUO

You can practice PC anytime, anyplace, and for any length of time. It may be the single greatest tool available to mankind! I covered how to do PC in Chapter 3, and mental imagery in Chapter 4. The following are examples of how to combine the two.

1.   When riding your horse, make pictures in your mind of your horse doing what you want, in relaxation and without force. If you can't make pictures, imagine how it feels in your body when your horse does what you want. Catch yourself if you're imagining what could go wrong. Your horse will pick up on that image or feeling and make it happen! Pre-cue your horse by visualizing what you want and then give the physical cue immediately after if he doesn't respond.

2.   When you're not riding your horse, make up stories in your mind of how you want things to be with your horse. Make these stories part of your PC sessions.

3.   Practice doing nothing mentally. Become comfortable with solitude and silence. This helps you create the pause when you work with your horse.

REMOVE UNNATURAL DISTRACTIONS

1.   Put down your cell phone—don't hold conversations or text while with your horse.

2.   Don't multitask, especially when trying to interact with horses. They require your **full** attention.

3.   Keep conversations with others to a minimum. Keep the conversation focused on your horse and what the two of you are doing.

4.   Prepare for natural distractions.

Notes:

You can't remove natural distractions from your environment. Honing your senses and learning to be present will help you gain peripheral vision and a soft awareness of what is going on around you. When you can do this, you may begin to notice potential dangers before they become a problem for you or your horse.

PC will help you focus your mind so that outside distractions don't rattle you. For example, if you're always scanning the environment for trouble with your conscious mind, your horse will be on alert and potentially spooky.

HAVING A CONVERSATION

A meaningful conversation can only happen after you have established a heart-to-heart and mind-to-mind communion. That is why I have walked you through all the previous exercises. Their purpose is to prepare you and your horse for conversation.

This is a simple overview of how to hold a conversation with your horse. The actual process can't be expressed in words, it has to be experienced. But the guidelines below will help you get started. They will give you things to consider.

CREATING A UNIVERSAL LANGUAGE— (USING YOUR INNER TRANSLATION DEVICE)

1. Complete the Preparation Routine as outlined above.

2. Establish pre-cues (pictures, feelings, thoughts, and emotions). Before you do something, make clear pictures in your mind of what you want your horse to do. (Horses and people understand pictures.)

3. Put feelings in your body of how you want it to feel (in you and the horse).

4. Imagine the emotion you want to feel when he or she does it right.

5. Talk to the horse energetically with your thoughts, heart energy, intentions, and emotions.

Notes:

Remember that thoughts change your emotions and your body's physiology—heart rate, reparation, GSR. Your horse senses these changes.

During a conversation, talk gently with pictures, feelings, seat, hands, and weight changes. Keep a positive and steady emotional state, even if things start going bad. Maintain relaxation in your body when your horse does what you want. Take frequent pauses so you can monitor your horse's reaction and level of understanding. Momentarily, make your body tense when your horse doesn't do what you're asking, and relax again immediately when he does it right.

If it feels like things are starting to go bad, focus on going forward and finding that place of rhythm and relaxation. Avoid getting into a fight.

To make progress, it's often necessary to push a horse up to the point of resistance and then back off. Backing off gives the horse a chance to understand that things don't stay hard.

Pushing a horse past his point of resistance and keeping him there for an extended period of time builds resentment. You begin having an argument that one or the other of you have to win. You are no longer having a conversation. Disagreements are part of conversation, arguments are not.

THE ART OF THE PAUSE

Pauses are critical. They help to prevent misunderstandings, and they resolve disagreements. The pause prevents arguments.

Pause **in your mind and body** to allow the horse to "tell" you the cause of his misunderstanding or disagreement.

Pause **in your mind and body** when you can't get the horse to do something right. This allows his mind time to process what happened. Make pictures in your mind of what you want him to do or how you want him to behave.

Reward your horse with your emotions, energy, and body when things go right. It's a way to tell him when he "got it."

Note:

Teach a horse maneuvers in the same way you might teach a young child to read. For example, before children can read, they must first learn the letters of the alphabet (how they look and sound). Then, they can start spelling easy words with the letters. After they learn the words, they can put them together into a sentence and then a paragraph. A horse must first learn the cue to move each individual part of its body (i.e., the letters) before you ask him to do a complex maneuver like a leg yield or side pass (i.e., the word). Putting a series of maneuvers together is the sentence or paragraph.

THE IMPORTANCE OF PROPER BREATHING

How often have you heard a riding instructor tell their student to breathe? Of all the things riders do, not breathing properly and effectively is common, if not epidemic. Improper breathing affects the ability of the muscles and brain to work efficiently—for both horse and rider. It can lead to tension, nervousness, and anxiety.

But here's the good news. Even though it's a hidden root cause of many riding or horse handling problems, it's also one of the easiest to fix. Before I give you some techniques for effective breathing, let's look at what happens when we don't breathe properly.

When a rider takes shallow breaths, or holds his/her breath for several seconds, muscle tension begins to build up in both the horse and rider. Rapid, shallow breathing can lead to hyperventilation and decreased carbon dioxide levels. As a result, blood vessels narrow and there is decreased blood flow to the brain. Less blood and oxygen to the brain can cause a variety of unpleasant and unwanted symptoms. These include lightheadedness, dizziness, confusion, and anxiety. The nervous system is also affected when there is too much oxygen. Calcium levels in the blood drop, resulting in numbness, tingling, spasms, or cramps in the muscles.[5]

I watched an Olympic gymnast warm up on the balance beam before her performance. She was working fluidly, but just before she mounted the beam, she took a shallow breath. As she breathed in, her shoulders rose (the first indication that she wasn't breathing deeply). The shallow breath caused her muscles to tighten and she fell off several times during her routine.

At a reining show, I observed a horse/rider team performing flawlessly in the warm-up arena. Just like the gymnast, the rider took a shallow breath just before entering the ring. I couldn't believe they were the same team. The horse and rider were stiff throughout the run. It seemed like the rider held that shallow breath throughout the entire ride because her face was beet red when she was done. I never saw her exhale and take another breath.

Proper breathing is easy to master. However, it does take some awareness and practice. Just telling yourself or a student to "breathe" is not the solution. Knowing **how** to breathe is the solution. We can quickly change our physiology and mindset through breathing. It is the one physiological function that we have conscious control over. When we learn to pay attention and control our breathing rate and method, we can instantly relax muscles, lower blood pressure, release endorphins (those natural pain relievers and mood enhancing chemicals), and cleanse the body of built up toxins.[6]

LEARNING HOW TO BREATHE EFFICIENTLY (FOR INCREASED HEALTH AND PERFORMANCE)[7]:

1. Calculate your normal respiration or breathing rate.

Using your phone or a stop watch, count the number of inhalations/exhalations you make in one minute. Count the inhalation and the exhalation as one full breath.

Twelve to 16 breaths per minute is considered normal. If you are making 25 to 40 breaths per minute, you are hyperventilating.[8] When you ride, strive to get down to around 5 to 10 breaths per minute. If you stay in that range, you'll remain relaxed.

2. Take a deep breath in, focusing on it going deep into your abdomen.

To make sure you're breathing deeply, place your hand on your stomach. If your hand rises and falls as you inhale and exhale, you are deep breathing. If there is no movement, you are shallow breathing or chest breathing.

3. Practice slow and deliberate breathing.

Breathe in slowly. Imagine the air filling up your entire chest cavity. Exhale slowly and completely. You can breathe in to the count of 5 and exhale to the count of 5 or 7. Just make sure your lungs feel empty before taking the next breath.

4-7-8 Breathing Technique[9]

If you are hyperventilating, anxious, fearful, or stressed, the 4-7-8 breathing technique is very helpful. Do this breathing exercise to quickly return to a relaxed body and a focused state of mind.

1. Place your tongue on the top of your mouth, just behind your front teeth. (Keep it there throughout the exercise. Make sure you are deep breathing, not chest breathing.)

2. Close your mouth and breathe in through your nose for a count of 4.

3. Hold your breath and count to 7.

4. Exhale completely through your mouth for a count of 8. As you empty your lungs, make a whoosh sound.

5. Repeat each of the previous steps four more times.

Practice!

Practice makes perfect. This statement is true for any kind of new skill. Practice will help you become a successful communicator with your horse on a new, deeper level. Trust that your horse understands the information you are sending and visualizing. Trust what you feel coming back to you from your horse is real. Experiment. Prove this to yourself through your own observations. You can do it!

Having a coach work with you when you begin your conscious communication practice is invaluable. A skilled coach can guide you through the process as you begin to experience energy flowing to and from your heart and throughout your body. A teacher can also provide feedback to let you know when you're running the energy in a way that a horse can understand. An experienced horse who is already open and expressive when he/she feels the energy can also be a terrific mirror to show you when you're connecting.

Although I made every attempt to clearly explain how to access the energetic field to improve your relationship with your horse, written words are not a substitute for experiential learning. Attending a clinic or symposium on energy connection and communication can catapult you into a whole new realm of understanding and skill in a very short time.

You may contact me at drsusanfay@gmail.com. For more information or to schedule a consultation or clinic in your area, visit my website, https://scienceandspiritofhorses.com. Like and Follow my Facebook page, *Science and Spirit of Horses*, to learn about upcoming events.

Epilogue

By now, you have probably come to realize that you haven't been given any riding techniques or training routines to get your horse to do what you want. Instead, this book is being presented from the horse's perspective. It's what horses might wish that humans knew, or how they wish humans would be around them. It's not similar to equine-assisted therapy or learning. That is a system to benefit humans. This is about what we humans can do that will benefit horses.

Except in the prologue, there was no mention of animal communication. In essence, we are all potentially animal communicators. This book should not be considered training in animal communication, although receiving information from animals is part of it. This manual should be considered an explanation of energetic communication. We all connect to and communicate with the entire energy field, whether we are aware of it or not. The goal is to become fully aware, and to learn to direct the energy and create a response in the way you consciously prefer, instead of by unconscious default.

Each being on this earth, and the earth itself, is made up of energy. It doesn't matter what form the energy takes—it doesn't even matter if that form is "alive" or "dead." After all, according to the first law of thermodynamics (i.e., the law of conservation of energy), energy can neither be created nor destroyed. It can only change form.

What you have learned in this book helps you connect with everything that exists in the energy field. With the entire energetic field at your disposal, the possibilities are limitless. You can venture outside "the box."

Here is list of things to remember or consider as you move forward. It's important to read and understand the philosophy, but it's more important to experiment and see how these concepts work for you. Experiencing something is much different from merely reading or hearing about it. Many of my students have shared with me that they have read about and understood my work, but when we actually apply the concepts to real life situations with their horses, they're excited and surprised. What happens when they practice what they've learned often leaves them speechless.

Suggestions

- Treat each interaction with your horse as something sacred.
- Set an intention of relaxation, love, joy, and caring each time you interact with horses.
- If it feels like you need to use force, pause. Explore the reason behind the resistance.
- Ride with intention, not tension.
- Prepare yourself (emotionally and physically) before any interaction with your horse.
- Make your mantra: Slow down and be present.
- Don't rely on treats as a training aid or reward.
- Reward your horse often with a light pat, your positive thoughts, and joyful energy.
- Keep a journal of your horse experiences—what worked and what didn't.
- Start noticing the difference between an energetic response and a behavioral response from your horse.
- Practice mental imagery often.
- Recognize when your self-talk is causing problems for you and your horse.

- Catch yourself before you create a label and story for a horse, unless it's a good label and a positive story.
- Find ways to recognize when you're in the present moment and when you're not.
- Minimize technological distractions when you interact with horses.
- Find ways to recognize when you are in the optimum brain wave pattern (Alpha) for interacting with horses.
- Treat each horse as an individual. One technique or training method doesn't work for all horses.
- Strive to make your communication with your horse clear and consistent.
- Use pre-cues. They help your horse prepare for what you're going to ask him to do.
- Stay open-minded and curious.
- The cure for resistance is relaxation—both mental and physical.
- Always try to work a horse in relaxation.
- Take time to teach your horse. Remember, a tired or stressed horse doesn't learn or retain information well.
- The source of power with your horse is your heart, not your logical mind.
- If you want a good ride, imagine it. Don't imagine what could go wrong.
- Learn and practice working with energy. Be patient, it may take time before you see results.
- Become consistent in your energy and your horse will begin to trust the "new" you.
- Understand that horses don't like to be around people whose energy is chaotic.
- Using energy is not a substitute for good horsemanship skills.
- Shut down your analytical and critical mind when riding or interacting with horses.

- You don't need any special tools or gadgets to work with energy. You only need **you**.
- Create clear intentions.
- Become comfortable with silence and solitude. The quiet place in your mind is where magic and creativity resides.
- Let go.
- Experiment.
- Seek help if you need it.
- Smile!
- Have Fun!

Conclusion

For almost 10 years, the idea of writing a book about my experiences with horses and energy work would occasionally pop up in my mind. Whenever this happened, I would immediately dismiss the thought. It seemed to me that I needed more credibility and science to back up my claims. Also, my human psychology background was leading me down an entirely different career track—one that took me far away from horses.

In early 2018, I decided to attend several dressage and natural horsemanship clinics in my area. As I watched riders struggle with their horses, I decided it was finally time to write this book. It occurred to me that a piece, or several pieces were missing from most human-horse interactions. They either weren't being taught, or clinicians/instructors weren't emphasizing the importance of these other pieces. Although it's always easy to critique from the sidelines, I began to see that I could offer something different and valuable to equestrians. The energy work, coupled with my dressage and psychology background, appeared to hold some of the missing pieces that could improve equestrians' connection and communication with their horse—and transform their relationship. A desire to improve the welfare of horses—and humans—ignited a passion in my heart that had been smoldering for years. It had finally turned into a calling that I could no longer ignore.

In my work with many equestrians over the years, I rarely told my students what I was doing on the inside. This was because I was still experimenting to see if my theories worked for others as well as they did for me. And I was scared that people would think I was a kook. Then, one glorious and enlightening day, I realized it wasn't about me at all; it was about making things better for horses.

I decided to be brave and tell people what I was actually doing. I arranged a small clinic at the ranch of a well-known and respected natural horsemanship trainer. During the clinic, some amazing things happened between several horses and riders, but the participants said nothing. No feedback whatsoever—until about a week later when one of them called me. As she shared stories about the difference in her horse, she cried . . . happy tears. I knew it wasn't what I had done that made such a difference; it was what **she** had done. I also realized that we had only scratched the surface of what is possible. After all, she had only activated a few of the concepts in this book!

Most good equestrians seek to learn all they can about horses. They genuinely want to do what's best for their horse. They attend clinics, take lessons, and read books. They practice humane training techniques, provide excellent care, and work hard to create a strong bond with their horse or horses. The desire of many people to be responsible and compassionate equestrians has helped fuel the natural horsemanship movement in this country.

The popularity of the natural horsemanship philosophy soared when Ray Hunt, Bill Dorrance, Tom Dorrance, Monte Roberts, John Lyons, and Buck Brannaman began sharing their training techniques and horsemanship principles through books, videos, and clinics. These horsemen advocated a gentler approach to horse-human interactions that would ensure a stronger bond and better cooperation from the horse.[1]

In reality, they were not the first to promote the use of less abusive horse training methods. The first "natural horseman" that made his mark on the horse world was a Greek named Xenophon. Around 400 BC, he wrote, *On Horsemanship*, a book in which he presented his philosophies on the care and humane training of horses.[2] The principles presented in his book have remained relevant for thousands of years. They are still practiced by many classical dressage trainers to this day.[3]

As the name seems to imply, if we follow the philosophies and practice the principles taught by natural horsemanship clinicians and classical dressage instructors, we can establish a better connection with our horse. Many of the original masters had a gift with horses, but they didn't—or couldn't—pass that gift down to all their students. They may have purposely kept what they did a secret, or they might not have realized that their true training effectiveness was coming from an entirely different place and set of skills. Their gift was perceived by those who observed them as a series of training techniques. Equestrians learned the physical training techniques of the masters, but they couldn't copy the invisible, energetic techniques the masters used that made them such exceptional horsemen. The essence of what the masters were really doing—*The Gift*—was missed. The gift was not merely some superior physical technique, it was also the ability to commune with a horse.

In this book, you have learned about the things you can do to assemble the pieces of your gift with horses. *The Gift* is about becoming more natural. It's the silence beyond whispers. It's the journey to becoming more horse-like. The more natural, authentic, and congruent you become, the more your horse understands you. After all, it's natural horsemanship, not natural horse. Horses are already quite skilled at being present and true to their nature. We can only hope to collaborate with horses in a way that allows them to maintain their dignity, health, and happiness.

Once you incorporate *The Gift* into your daily interactions with your horse, you may actually become a *supernatural* horseman! You'll be using all the abilities that humans were born with—the ones that have been ignored or obscured by technology.

If you take the leap off the cliff into a new way of thinking about horse-human interactions, you may not be able to go back to your old ways. Over the cliff is a new way of perceiving and being in the world. If you jump, your paradigm will shift. Although the old ways were good, you'll understand how interactions with your horse can be even better. You may feel alone and misunderstood at first, but know that there are others like you out there. I'm not the only one teaching these principles. There's enough room for more to join us.

Dr. Wayne Dyer talked about "the shift," a way to change yourself so that you can discover spiritual connectedness and your true potential.[4] In this book, I have expanded the concept of *The Shift* to include our horses. You need not worry about trying to shift others, just focus on yourself and your horse. When others see the positive changes in you and your horse, they may seek to shift as well. Often when we change ourselves, we change others as well. There may be many more that jump off the cliff and join us—in the sacred space!

This book was written from my heart. In my heart is a love for horses. I can't recall a time that horses have not been a part of my being—my essence. In my heart, I feel that it's important for people to hear or read about the concepts contained in the pages of this book—not for my sake, but for the sake of the horse.

I often hear horse owners or trainers tell stories of their "once in a lifetime horse." Now you know that every horse has the potential to be a once in a lifetime horse. What we should strive to be is our horse's once in a lifetime human.

Horses gift us with their power, beauty, grace, and wisdom. Becoming better humans can be our gift to them.

References

Introduction

[1] Perry, W. (2009, July). One giant leap. *Smithsonian National Portrait Gallery.* Retrieved from www.npg.si.edu/blog/one-giant-leap-apollo-11

Chapter 2: Getting on the Same Wavelength

[1] Schoen, A. E. (2015). *The compassionate equestrian: 25 principles to live by when caring for and working with horses.* North Pomfret, VT: Trafalgar Square.

[2] NOVA. (2003). *What drives earth's magnetic field?* Retrieved from https://www.pbs.org/wgbh/nova/magnetic/reve-drives.html

[3] Goldman, J. G. (2016, April 8). Re: Can we sense invisible magnetic fields? [Web log message]. Retrieved from www.bc.com/future/story/20160408-can-we-sense-invisible-magnetic-fields

[4] Mayo Clinic. (n.d.). *Electrocardiogram (ECG or EKG).* Retrieved from https://www.mayoclinic.org/tests-procedures/ekg/about/pac-20384983

[5] Mayo Clinic. (n.d.). *EEG (electroencephalogram).* Retrieved from https://www.mayoclinic.org/tests-procedures/eeg/about/pac-20393875

[6] Villarejo, M. V., Zapirain, B. G., & Zorrillo, A. M. (2012). A stress sensor based on galvanic skin response (GSR controlled by ZigBee. *Sensors, 12*(5), 6075-6101. Retrieved from https://www.ncbi.nim.gov/pms/articles/PMC3386730/

[7] Auster, H-U. (2008). How to measure earth's magnetic field. *Physics Today, 61*(2), 76. Retrieved from https://doi.org/10/1063/1.2883919

[8] Goldman (2016)

[9] Smith, William L. (1992). The human electromagnetic energy field: Its relationship to interpersonal communication. *Journal of Theoretics, 4*(2). Retrieved from www.journaloftheoretics.com/articles/4-2/Smith.htm

181

[10] The Editors of Encyclopedia Britannica. (1988, July 20). *Animal magnetism.* Retrieved from https://www.britannica.com/science/animal-magnetism

[11] McKay, B. (2017). *Your energy signature.* Retrieved from https://www.amazon.com/You-Energy-Signature-Professionals-Creating-ebook/dp/B074BGZDT7

[12] Australian Spinal Research Foundation. (2016, July 26). Re: The three brains: Why your head, heart, and gut sometimes conflict [Web log message]. Retrieved from https://wpinalresearch.com.au/three-brains-head-heart-gut-sometimes-conflict/

[13] https://www.heartmath.org/research/science-of-the-heart-brain-communication/

[14] Mysoor, A. (2017, February 2). Re: The science behind intuition and how you can use it to get ahead at work [Web log message]. https://www.forbes.com/sites/alexandramysoor/2017/02/02/the-science-behind-intuition-and-how-you-can-use-it-to-get-ahead-at-work/#6fdc7af9239f

[15] Gigerenzer, G. (2007) *Gut feelings: The intelligence of the unconscious.* New York, NY: The Penguin Group.

[16] McCraty, R. (2003). *The energetic heart: Bioelectromagnetic interaction within and between people.* HeartMath Research Center, Institute of HeartMath. Retrieved from https://www.heartmath.org

[17] McCraty, R., & Deyhle, A. (2016). *The science of interconnectivity: Exploring the human-earth connection.* HeartMath Research Center - Global Coherence Initiative. Retrieved from https://www.heartmath.org

[18] McCraty (2003)

[19] Childre, D., & Martin, H. (1999). Magnetometer. This instrument can measure the heart's electromagnetic energy up to 8-10 feet away from the heart. *The HeartMath Solution.* San Francisco, CA: Harper.

[20] McCraty (2003)

[21] McCraty (2003)

[22] Mistral, K. (2014, January 21). Re: Measuring the emotional bond between horses and humans [Web log message]. Retrieved from https://www.habitatforhorses.org/measuring-the-emotional-bond-between-horses-and-humans/

[23] Childre, D., & Martin, H. (1999). *The HeartMath solution.* San Francisco, CA: HarperSanFrancisco.

[24] Mistral (2014)

[25] McCraty, R., & Childre, D. (2014). *The intuitive heart: Accessing inner guidance to raise our consciousness baseline.* Boulder Creek, CA: HeartMath Research Center, Institute of HeartMath. Retrieved from http://www.heartmath.org

[26] McCraty (2003)

[27] McCraty, R. & Deyhle, A. (2016). *The science of interconnectivity: Exploring the human-earth connection.* Boulder Creek, CA: HeartMath Institute. Retrieved from http://www.heartmath.org

[28] McCraty and Deyhle (2016)

[29] emWave. www.emwave.com

[30] McCraty and Childre (2014)

[31] Cade, M. C., & Coxhead, N. (1989). *The awakened mind: Biofeedback and the development of higher states of awareness.* Great Britain: Element Books

[32] Doidge, N. (2015). *The brain's way of healing.* New York, NY: The Penguin Group

[33] Cade and Coxhead (1989)

[34] Cade and Coxhead (1989)

[35] Doidge (2015)

[36] Doidge (2015)

[37] Siegel, D. J. (2014, February 4). Pruning, myelination, and the remodeling adolescent brain. *Psychology Today.* Retrieved from

https://www.psychologytoday.com/us/blog/inspire-rewire/201402/pruning-myelination-and-the-remodeling-adolescent-brain

[38] Siegel (2014)

[39] The Guardian. (2012, February 28). Re: How many neurons make a human brain? Billions fewer than we thought [Web log message]. Retrieved from https://www.theguardian.com/science/blog/2012/feb/28/how-many-neurons-human-brain

[40] Mayo Clinic. (n.d.). EEG (electroencephalogram). Retrieved from https://www.mayoclinic.org/tests-procedures/eeg/about/pac-20393875

[41] Cade and Coxhead (1989)

[42] Cade and Coxhead (1989)

[43] Cade and Coxhead (1989)

[44] Siegel, D. J. (2007). *The mindful brain: Reflection and attunement in the cultivation of well-being.* New York, NY: W. W. Norton & Company

[45] Levitin, D. J. (2014). *An organized mind.* New York, NY: The Penguin Group

[46] Neilsen, J. A., Zielinski, B. A., Ferguson, M. A., Lainhart, J. E., & Anderson, J. S. (2013). An evaluation of the left-brain vs. right-brain hypothesis with resting state functional connectivity magnetic resonance imaging. *PLoS ONE, 8*(8): e71275. Retrieved from https://doi.org/10.1371/journal.pone.0071275

[47] Pietrangelo, A. (2017, January 18). Re: Left brain vs. right brain: What does this mean for me? [Web log message]. Retrieved from https://www.healthline.com/health/left-brain-vs-right-brain

[48] Pietrangelo (2017, January 18)

[49] Brenton, L. (2016, April 5). Re: 10 tips to develop both sides of your brain [Web log message]. Retrieved from https://www.dumblittleman.com/10-tips-develop-sides-brain/

[50] Kritsky, G., & Mader, D. (2010). Leonardo's insects. *American Entomologist, Fall 2010.* Retrieved from https://academic.oup.com/ae/article-abstract/56/3/178/2364785

[51] David, L. (2007, January 17). Re: "Attribution Theory (Weiner). *Learning Theories*. Retrieved from https://www.learning-theories/weiners-attribution-theory.html

[52] Weiner, B. (1974). *Achievement motivation and attribution theory*. Morristown, NJ: General Learning Press

[53] David (2007)

[54] Fetlock, P. E. (1985). Accountability: A social check on the Fundamental Attribution Error. *Social Psychology Quarterly, 48*(3), 227-236. Retrieved from www.jstor.org/Fri June 17 17:13:54 2005

[55] Kanai, R., Walsh, V., & Tseng, C. (2010). Subjective discriminability of invisibility: A framework for distinguishing perceptual and attentional failures of awareness. *Consciousness and Cognition (2010).* doi:10.1016/j.concog.2010.06.003

[56] Carpenter, S. (2001). Sights unseen. *Monitor, 32*(4), 54. Retrieved from www.pa.org/monitor/apr01/blindness.aspx

Chapter 3: The Thought-full and Emotional Human

[1] MindBodyVortex. (2016, August 24). The ancient art of 'no mind' and the benefits of modern practice. Retrieved from http://www.mindbodyvortex.com/the-ancient-art-of-no-mind-and-the-benefits-of-modern-practice/

[2] Suzuki, S. (2010). *Zen mind, beginner's mind: Informal talks on Zen meditation and practice*. Boston & London: Shambhala.

[3] Netherton, S. (2015, April 28). Gastric ulcers: Common in performance horses, foals. Retrieved from https://vetmed.illinois.edu/pet_column/equine_ulcers/

[4] Delgado, M. & Pignon, F. (2013). *Building a life together: You and your horse.* North Pomfret, VT: Trafalgar Square Books

[5] Bishop, W. H. (2012, July 12). The thoughts, emotions, and behaviors triangle. Retrieved from http://www.thoughtsfroma-therpist.com/2012/07/12/thoughts-emotions-behaviors-triangle/

[6] Cassidy, S. (n.d.). "Whether you think you can, or you think you can't-you're right. Retrieved from https://www.heacademy.ac.uk/"whether-you-think-you-can-or-you-think-you-cant-youre-right"

Chapter 4: Image that . . .

[1] Stiller, B. [Director]. (2013). *The secret life of Walter Mitty* [DVD]. Available from https://www.imdb.com/title/tt0359950

[2] Weinberg, R. (2008). Does imagery work? Effect on performance and mental skills. *Journal of Imagery Research in Sport and Physical Activity, 3*(1), ISSN (Online) 1932-01091. doi:10.2202/1932/0191.1025

[3] Rosslyn, S. M., Ganis, G., & Thompson, W. L. (2001). Neural foundations of imagery. *Nature Reviews Neuroscience, 2,* 635-642. Retrieved from www.nature.com/reviews/neuro

[4] Rosslyn, et, al. (2001)

[5] Doidge, N. (2015). *The brain's way of healing: Remarkable discoveries and recoveries from the frontiers of neuroplasticity.* New York, New York: A Penguin Random House Company

[6] Ehrsson, H. H., Geyer, S., & Naito, E. (2003). Imagery of voluntary movement of fingers, toes, and tongue activities corresponding body-part: Specific motor representations. *Journal of Neurophysiology, 90,* 3304-3316 doi: 10/1152/jn.01113.2002

[7] Shackell, E. M., & Standing, L. (2007). Mind over matter: Mental training increases physical strength. *North American Journal of Psychology, 9*(1), 189-200.

[8] Brouziyne, M., & Molinaro, C. (2005). Mental imagery combined with physical practice of approach shots for golf beginners. *Perceptual and Motor Skills, 101*(1), 203-211 https://doi.org/10/2466/pms.101.1.203-211

[9] Brouziyne and Molinaro (2005)

[10] Shen, J. (2013, June 29). Re: The science of practice: What happens when you learn a new skill [Web log message]. Retrieved from https://lifehacker.com/the-science-of-practice-what-happens-when-you-learn-a--510255025

[11] Van Gog, T., Paas, F., Marcus, N., Ayres, P., & Sweller, J. (2009). The mirror-neuron system and observational learning: Implications for the effectiveness of dynamic visualization. *Educational Psychology Review, 21*, 21-30. Retrieved from wwwlspringerlink.co

[12] Par, N. (2008). The infant mirror neuron system studied with high density EEG. *Social Neuroscience, 3*(3-4). 334-347. doi:10.1080/17470910701563665

[13] Bishop, W. H. (2012, July 12). Re: The thoughts, emotions, and behaviors triangle [Web log message]. Retrieved from http://www.thoughtsfroma-therpist.com/2012/07/12/thoughts-emotions-behaviors-triangle/

[14] Purves, D., Augustine, G. J., Fitzpatrick, D., Katz, L. C., LaMania, A-S., McNamara, J. O., & Williams, S. M. (Editors). (2001). *Neuroscience, 2nd edition.* Sunderland, MA: Sinauer Associates

[15] MIT Media Laboratory (n.d.). Galvanic skin response. Retrieved from https://www.media.mit.edu/galvactivator/faw.html

[16] Purves, et al. (2001)

[17] Rossman, M. L. ((2016). The benefits of imagery. *Psych Central.* Retrieved from https://psychcentral.com/lib/the-benefits-of-imagery/

[18] Limbach, A. (2017, August 25). Re: The benefits of making visualization meditation a part of our daily routine [Web log message]. Retrieved from https://www.mindbodygrccn.com/articles/the-benefits-making-visualization-meditation-a-part-of-your-daily-routine

Chapter 5: Clearing the Air(waves): Intentions and Pre-Cues

[1] Parisi, G., Cavagna, A., Cimarelli, A., Giardina, I., Santagati, R., Stefanini, F., & Viale, M. (2010). Scale-free correlations in starling flocks. *Proceedings of the National Academy of Sciences, 107*(24). Retrieved from https://doi.org/10.1073/pnas.1005766107

[2] Parisi, et al. (2010).

[3] Keim, B. (2010, June 16). Amazing starling flocks are flying avalanches Web blog message]. Retrieved from https://www.wired.com/2010/06/starling-physics

4 Young, G. F., Scardovi, L., Cavagna, A., Giardina, I., & Leonard, N. E. (2013). Starling flock networks manage uncertainty in consensus at low cost. *PLoS Computational Biology, 9*(1): e1002894. Retrieved from https://doi.org/10.1371/journal.pcbi.1002894

Chapter 6: Coming to your Senses

1 Shyamalan, M. N. [Director]. (1999). *The sixth sense* [DVD]. Available from https://www.imbd.com/title/tt0167404

2 Klosowski, T. (2012, November 12). Re: How to develop Sherlock Holmes-like powers of observation and deduction [Web log message]. Retrieved from https://lifehacker.com/5960811/how-to-develop-sherlock-holmes-like-powers-of-observation-and-deduction

3 Markowsky, G. (2017). *Information theory*. Retrieved from https://britannica.com/science/information-theory/Physiology

4 DiSalvo, D. (2013, June 22). *Your brain sees even when you don't*. Retrieved from https://www.forbes.com/sites/daviddisalvo/2013/06/22/your-brain-sees-even-when-you-dont/#34ac94ad116a

5 Mack, A., & Rock, I. (1998). *Inattentional blindness*. Retrieved from https://doi.org.10.1016/S1364-6613(98)01244-3

6 Carpenter, S. (2001). Sights unseen. *Monitor, 32*(4), 54. Retrieved from www.pa.org/monitor/apr01/blindness.aspx

7 Mack and Rock (1998)

8 Klosowski (2012)

9 Walker, E. (2014, October 27). Re: Proprioception: Your sixth sense. Why movement and sensation are inextricably linked [Web log message]. Retrieved from https://helix.northwestern.edu/article/proprioception-your-sixth-sense

10 Ince, J. (2011, December 15). Re: The sixth sense: Thermoception [Web log message]. Retrieved from https://themedschoolproject.wordpress.com/2011/12/15/the-sixth-sense-thermoception/

11 Tracy, D. W. Jr. (2017). Nociception. *Primer, 27*(4), PR129-R133. doi:https://doi.org/10/1016/j.cub.2017.01.037

[12] Dubin, A. E., & Patapoutian, A. (2010). Nociceptors: The sensors of the pain pathway. *Journal of Clinical Investigation, 120*(11), 3760-3773. doi: 10/1172/JC142843

[13] Nordmann, G. C., Hochstoeger, T., & Keays, D. A. (2017). Magnetoreception: A sense without a receptor. *PLoS Biology, 15*(10), e2003234. https://doi.org/10.1371/journal.pbio.2003234

[14] Solov'yov, I., & Schulman, K. (n.d.). *Crypto chrome and magnetic sensing: Animal magnetoreception.* Retrieved from https://www.ks.uiuc.edu/Research/cryptochrome/

[15] Ince, J. (2011, November 26). Re: The sixth sense: Equilibrioception [Web log message]. Retrieved from https://themedschoolproject.wordpress.com/2011/11/26/the-sixth-sense-equilibrioception/

[16] Piper, A. (2018). *Humans have more than 5 senses. Here they are...* Retrieved from twentytwowords.com/humans-have-more-than-5-senses-here-they-are

[17] Hopkins, M. (2017). *Healing, awakening wisdom in the sacred feminine from the ancient Egyptians.* Retrieved from https://sacredfeminineawakening.com/healing-awakening-wisdom-sacred-feminine-ancient-egyptians/

[18] Ramis, H. [Director]. (1993). *Groundhog day* [DVD].

Chapter 7: Expectations, Labels, and Stories

[1] Layton, J. (2018). *How fear works: Flight or fright.* Retrieved from https://science.howstuffworks.com/life/inside-the-mind/emotions/fear2.htm

[2] Greene, B., & Comerford, P. (2009, September 24). Re: Horse fight vs horse instinct [Web log message]. Retrieved from http://articles.exension.org/pages/23342/horse-fight-vs-flight-instinct

[3] Krupic, J. (2017). Wire together, fire apart. *Science, 357*(6355), 974-975. doi: 10/1126/science.aao4159

[4] Ghosh, S. (n.d.). *Physiology of emotion.* Retrieved from https://slideshare.net/mobile/shaan_47/physiology-of-emotion-5651975

[5] Smith, A. V., Proops, L. Grounds, K., Wathan, J., & McComb, K. (2016). Functionally relevant responses to human facial expression of emotion in the domestic horse (Equus cabals). *Biology Letters 12*(2015097). http://ds.doi.org/10.1098/rsbl.2015.0907

[6] Merkies, K., Sievers, A., Zakrajsek, E., MacGregor, H., Bergeron, R., & Konig van Borstel, U. (2014). Preliminary results suggest an influence of psychological and physiological stress in human on horse heart rate and behavior. *Journal of Veterinary Behavior: Clinical Applications and Research, 9*(5), 242-247. http://dx.doi.org/10.1016/j.jveb.2014,06.003

[7] Hatzigeorgiadis, A., Zourbanos, N., Galanis, E., & Theodorakis, Y. (2011). Self-talk and sports performance: A meta-analysis. *Perspectives on Psychological Science, 6*(4) 348-356. doi:10/1177/1745691611413136

[8] Jantz, G. (2016, May 16). Re: The power of positive self-talk [Web log message]. Retrieved from https://www.psychologytoday.com/us/blog/hope-relationships/201605/-the-power-of-positive-self-talk

[9] Gottschall, J. (2013). *The storytelling animal: How stories make us human*. Retrieved from https://hispaculture.org/book/452679925/download-the-storytelling-animal-houghton-mifflin-harcourt.pdf

[10] Hsu, J. (2008). The secrets of storytelling: Our love for telling tales reveals the working of the mind. *Scientific American Mind, 19*(4) 15552284. Retrieved from https://pdfs.semanticscholar.org/83ef/ba087fc7016fedd9b9a9ec501a62f97a7aa7.pdf

[11] Now Novel (n.d.). Re: What makes a good story? 10 elements [Web log message]. Retrieved from https://www.nownovel.com/blog/what-makes-a-good-story/

[12] Calch, A. (2017, July 10). Re: 7 amazing ways how writing impacts your brain for good [Web log message]. Retrieved from https://medium.com/mindvalley/7-amazing-ways-how-writing-impacts-your-brain-for-good-77327a758679

Chapter 9: Attitude is Everything

[1] McLeod, S. A. (2014). *Attitudes and behavior*. Retrieved from https://www.simplypsychology.org/articles/html

[2] Sharma, H. (2014, August 1). Re: Attitude makes habit, habit makes character and character makes a man [Web log message]. Retrieved from http://www.careerride.com/view/attitude-makes-habit-habit-makes-character-and-character-makes-a-man-15810.aspx

[3] Ray, O. (2004). How the mind hurts and heals the body. *American Psychologist, 59*(1), 29-40. doi: 10/1037/0003-006X.59.1.29

[4] McLeod, S. A. (2015). *Cognitive behavioral therapy.* Retrieved from http://simplypsychology.org/cognitive-therapy.html

[5] Sherman, J. (2010, June 13). Re: Total control vs no control theory of emotions: Can you control your emotions or not? [Web log message]. Retrieved from http://www.psychlogytoday.com/us/blog/ambitamy/201006/total-control-vs-no-control-theory-emotions-can-you-control-your-emotions-or-not

[6] Whitbourne, S. K. (2015). Re: 5 ways to get your unwanted emotions under control: Anger, disappointment, and resentments can't be erased. But they can be evaded [Web log message]. Retrieved from http://psychologytoday.com/us/blog/fullfillment-any-age/201502/5-ways-to-get-your-unwanted-emotions-under-control

Chapter 10: Presence - The Colossal Superpower

[1] Tolle, E. (2017). Becoming a teacher of presence: Bringing awareness to the service of others [CD]. Retrieved from https://www.audible.com/pd/Religion-Spirituality/Becoming-a-Teacher-of-Presence-Audiobook/B072JHNRN3

[2] MindValley (n.d.). Re: Everything you want to know about mindfulness meditation [Web log message]. Retrieved from https://blog.mindvalley.com/mindfulness-meditation

[3] Wickens, C. D., Gutzwiller, R. S., & Sanataria, A. (2015). Discrete task switching in overload: A meta-analysis and a model. *International Journal of Human-Computer Studies, 79*, 79-84. doi: 10/1016/j/ijhcs.2015.01.002

[4] Wiens, K. (2017, December 21). Re: Break the cycle of stress and distraction by using your emotional intelligence [Web log message]. Retrieved from https://www.hbr.org/2017/12/break-the-cycle-of-stress-and-distraction-by-using-your-emotional-intelligence

[5] Cooper, B. B. (2017, February 14). Re: Quiet doesn't cut it: Why your brain might work better in silence [Web log message]. Retrieved from https://www.fastcompany.com/3068168/quiet-doesnt-cut-it-why-your-brain-might-work-better-in-silence

[6] Gross, D. (2014, August 21). Re: This is your brain on silence: Contrary to popular belief, peace and quiet is all about the noise in your head [Web log message]. Retrieved from https://www.nautil.us/issue/16/nothingness/this-is-your-brain-on-silence

Chapter 11: The Lost Art of Conversation

[1] Spiritual Science (2015, March 5). *A conversation is so much more than words. A conversation is eyes, smiles, and the silences between words.* Annika Thor. Retrieved from https://stardust-seedling.tumblr.com/post/112772487673/a-conversation-is-so-much-more-tan-words-a

[2] Anand, V. (2017, July 19). Re: Universal language: 10 types of human communication [Web log message]. Retrieved from http://www.look4ward.co.uk/lifestyle/universal-language-10-types-of-human-communication

[3] Arnold, C. (2014). *How do horses communicate? New signals found.* Retrieved from https://news.nationalgeographic.com/news/2014/08/horse-communication-ears

[4] Talbot, W. (2017, August 31). Re: How horses communicate with their ears, eyes and mouth [Web log message]. Retrieved from https://www.horsedialog.co.uk/health/horses-communicate

[5] Richter, R. (2014, November 13). Re: 5 questions: Temple Grandin discusses autism, animal communication [Web log message]. Retrieved from http://med.stanford.edu/news/all-news/2014/11/5-questions-temple-grandin-discusses-autism-animal-communication.html

[6] Brown, J. (2013, January 21). Re: Connection vs conversation [Web log message]. Retrieved from https://www.soicalmediatoday.com/content/connection-vs-conversation

[7] Smith, V. A., Proops, L., Grounds, K., Wathan, J., Scott, S. K., & McComb, K. (2018). Domestic horses (*Equus caballus*) discriminate between negative and

positive human nonverbal vocalizations. *Scientific Reports, 8*(13952). https://doi.org/10.1038/s41598-018-30777-z

[8] Smith, V. A., Proops, L., Grounds, K., Wathan, J., & McComb, K. (2016). Punctually relevant responses to human facial expressions of emotion in the domestic horse (*Equus caballus*). *Biology Letters.* http://dx.doi.org?10.1098/rsbi.2015.0907

[9] Nakamura, K., Takimoto-Inose, A., & Hasegawa, T. (2018). Cross-modal perception of human emotion in domestic horses (*Equus caballus*). *Scientific Reports, 8*(8660). https://doi.org/10.1038/s41598/s41598-018-26892-6

[10] White, S. (2015). *Sharon White: Become a self-confident leader for your horse.* Retrieved from https://practicalhorsemanmag.com/training/self-confident-leader-27845

[11] BBC (n.d.). Re: The structures of control in the Nazi state [Web log message]. Retrieved from http://www.bbc.co.uk/schools/gcsebitesize/history/mwh/germany/controlstructurerev_print.shtml

[12] Chris, J. (2015, September 4). Re: 5 Martin Luther King Jr leadership style axioms [Web log message]. Retrieved from www.josephchris.com/5-martin-luther-king-jr-leadership-style-axioms

[13] Moore, K. (2011, August 11). Re: Two lessons from India's greater leader–Gandhi [Web log message]. Retrieved from https://www.forbes.com/sites/karlmoore/2011/08/22/2-lessons-from-indiasgreatest-leader-gandhi/#56948e2155ec

[14] loveandlogic.com

Chapter 12: Connecting all the Pieces

[1] Oliveria, N. (1988). *Reflections on equestrian art.* London, England: J.A. Allen

[2] Straightness Training. (n.d.). *The brain of the horse.* Retrieved from: http://straightnesstraining.com/the-horse/the-mind-of-the-horse/the-brain-of-the-horse/

[3] Zettl, W. (1998). *Dressage in harmony.* Boonsboro, MD: Half Halt Press, Inc.

[4]Zettl (1998)

[5]Ansgar, C., Muller, A., Doberenz, S., Kim, S., Meuret, A. A., Wollburg, E., & Roth, W. T. (2007). Psychophysiological effects of breathing instruction for stress management. *Applied Psychophysiology Biofeedback, 32*(89-98). doi: 10/1007/s10484-007-9034-xAnsgar

[6]W. E. (2017). Re: 5 benefits of deep breathing exercises [Web log message]. Retrieved from https://livingthenourishedlife.com/5-ways-youll-benefit-from-daily-deep/

[7]Lin, I. M., Tai, L.Y., & Fan, S. Y. (2014). Breathing at a rate of 5.5 breaths per minute with equal inhalation-to-exhalation ratio increases heart rate variability. *International Journal of Psychophysiology, 91*(3), 206-211. doi:10.1016/j.ijpsycho.3013.12.006

[8]Cleveland Clinic (n.d.). *Vital signs*. Retrieved from https://my.clevelandclinic.org/health/articles/10881-vital-signs

[9]The Spire Wellness Team (2018, April 28). Re: How to use the 4-7-8 breathing technique to reduce stress [Web log message]. Retrieved from https://blog.spire.io/2018/04/28/4-7-8

Conclusion

[1]Hamilton, A. J. (2010). *A history of natural horsemanship: From ancient times to the present*. Rancho Bosque, LLC. Retrieved from www.zenmindzenhorse.com/PDFs/ANaturalHistoryofHorsemanship.pdf

[2]Xenophon (author), Henry G. Dakyns (Translator). (2008). *On Horsemanship*. Retrieved from https://www.gutenberg.org/files/1176/1176-h/1176-h.htm

[3]Knipp, J. (2013, August). *The art of classic dressage training: A top judge reminds us to stick to the classical principles in our training*. Retrieved from https://dressagetoday.com/instruction/the-art-of-classic-dressage-training

[4]Dyer, W. W. (2010). The shift: Taking your life from ambition to meaning. United States: Hay House, Inc.

Book and Image Credits

BOOK CREDITS

Front and rear cover photos by Karen L. Duplantis, Fiore Photography
Cover design by Ellen Storeim, Ellen Kendrick Creative Inc.
Book Layout ©2017 BookDesignTemplates.com
Editing by Tabitha Roberts-Carver
Published by Selenite Press, Ltd., Elbert, Colorado

IMAGE CREDITS

PREFACE
Foals in field-Susan Fay
Running horses-mattknoth
(animalphotos.info/a/2007/12/29/galloping-herd-of-horses-in-dried-grass-field/"><img)
Horse heads-Colourbox.com
CHAPTER 1
Cattle guard-Susan Fay
Fireplace-Colourbox.com
Horse in snow-Thomas Tucker on Unsplash
CHAPTER 2
Rearing horse-Onepixel.com
Woman riding horse-Onepixel.com
Figure 1: Heart waves-Susan Fay
EmWave figure-Susan Fay
Neurons-Colourbox.com
EEG-Colourbox.com
Paul and Sally-Dylan Nolte on Unsplash

Permission to use images in this book obtained from the photographer or company that holds the copyright. Documentation on file with Dr. Susan Fay.

Index

Author

SUSAN D. FAY, PHD

Dr. Susan Fay has been a professional musician, environmental scientist, rancher, horse trainer, sport performance consultant, hypnotherapist, and psychological health researcher. Susan bred and trained Morgan horses for over 20 years and accumulated world and national championships in Morgan dressage. She also showed her horses in open USDF dressage competitions, receiving several regional championships and a USEF Horse of the Year award. She has a bachelors and master's degree in Environmental Science and a PhD in Psychology. Dr. Fay's diverse background enables her to draw on a broad range of experiences and knowledge to arrive at innovative ways to improve horse-human and human-human relationships.

Dr. Fay is devoted to enhancing the lives of both horses and people. Through experiential learning and stories, Susan guides her students to an understanding of how animals (including humans) energetically connect and communicate. She teaches equestrians the concepts presented in this book through seminars, clinics, and private sessions.

Susan lives on a small ranch in Colorado. She is joyfully surrounded by nature and her 7 horses, 2 dogs, and a barn full of cats.

For information on upcoming events, Like and Follow Dr. Fay's Facebook page, *Science and Spirit of Horses*. If you want more information, or wish to schedule a consultation or clinic with her, send a request to: drsusanfay@gmail.com or visit https://scienceandspiritofhorses.com

Printed in Great Britain
by Amazon

58959302R00131